HOW TO START
A HOME-BASED
CARPENTRY BUSINESS

HOW TO START A HOME-BASED CARPENTRY BUSINESS

2nd edition

by Charles Self

The Globe Pequot Press

Old Saybrook, Connecticut

Copyright © 1995, 1997 by Charles Self

Cover and text design by Nancy Freeborn

Library of Congress Cataloging-in-Publication Data is available.

ISBN 0-7627-0065-3

Manufactured in the United States of America
Second Edition/First Printing

CONTENTS

INTRODUCTION

Today there are more reasons than ever for starting a business at home: first, and probably foremost, is the flexibility that working from your own home gives you. Today's electronic machines make a home-based carpentry business more feasible. Your office is covered, regardless of whether someone is around to tend the phone while you're out sawing wood and driving nails or doing other necessary things. In addition, working at home has become more acceptable as more and more people find they *can* go home again—to work. Electronics may eventually allow us to go back to the village concept, with almost everything a community needs available from people working from their homes, or nearby shops.

There are other considerations: Many companies are downsizing, and the economy is still taking some shallow breaths. Building starts are up as I write this, however, and will probably remain there for some time to come. That means there's another good reason for jumping off the precipice at this time: plenty of work for those who know how to get it.

As a craftsman or craftswoman, you're already more independent than most. It probably hasn't been all that long since you loaded your tools and took your skills from one contractor to another because you were displeased over something—maybe the tool policy or the condition of the portable toilets on the job sites. Or the next guy down the block may just have had some greener grass for you—a more complex, more interesting structure to complete. Such independence of mind is often well rewarded by opening your own business, where an ability to think and act for yourself is a greater help than in many other jobs.

With your own small carpentry/cabinetry or building business, you'll probably have much more fun, and may well turn out better work than you would working for someone else. You'll also make more money in a good year.

If you do it right, have a little luck, and are willing to work very hard, then working out of an office at home will suit for you, and will pay dividends. Those dividends can be large.

There are also some drawbacks. The IRS is enforcing ever more restrictive regulations regarding the home workplace. And interest rates are rising, which means that sooner or later building starts will slow until the rates homeowners pay start to drop again.

In addition, you will probably miss the "safety net" you once enjoyed. Once the paycheck is gone, so are the other benefits—retirement, health insurance, company vehicles, out-of-town expenses. There is also the simple fact that a person working for someone else simply does not have to work as hard as the person who works for himself or herself and has no one around to take up the slack.

Setting up a carpentry business involves one skill that you may have to learn from scratch—how to market your business. Answering the phone with "Yeah?" isn't apt to scare off droves of customers, as it might in a more sales-oriented business. But you will need to switch to more of a marketing mode. Finding leads to possible customers and letting those customers know you're skilled, available, and charge reasonable prices is particularly important at the start, before you've had time to build a really solid rep as a good worker who brings jobs in on time.

It is worth it? Is it worth it for you? That's what the early part book of this is all about. You'll also read about the mechanics of outfitting the office, bookkeeping, hiring and firing, paying taxes, and dealing with building codes.

Examine all the requirements for becoming an independent carpenter/builder. You may change your life.

CHAPTER ONE

IS THIS FOR YOU?

ome Office Computing magazine states that in 1995, 5.2 million new home offices started up. Many of those businesses did not make it. One of the major reasons businesses fail is under-capitalization at the start-up, but another is the simple fact that the person opening the business hasn't prepared herself or himself to successfully set up and operate it.

CARPENTRY FROM THE HOME

A carpentry business can be run from the home as successfully as any other, even though the basic work is carried out in the field. In fact, it is among the most common home-based businesses. Starting a carpentry business is more a matter of having the right tools and transportation than the right office. As little as 40 or 50 square feet will serve very well as a base for your business. You need room for a desk, file cabinet, plans bucket, and wastebasket. Add a phone line and a chair, and you're just about set. Of course, the list of tools needed to start a carpentry business is long, and some tools are quite costly.

A cabinetry business requires more space to accommodate large equipment, and any developing carpentry business is going to need more space as the business succeeds. You'll have to hire office personnel eventually, and maybe several crews to finish your work.

You may be the world's greatest cabinetmaker or lead carpenter—what my old boss called a crew boss—but until you master the niggling details of office work and of the jobs you undertake, you're going to be balancing on the cutting edge of failure.

PERSONALITY

The absolute first step in making sure you're going to get that business up and running and keep it functioning happily is for you to have the right type of personality. If you prefer to kick back and let things ride, if getting there is less than half the fun, and if doing a good job in less time than allotted doesn't seem like much, then forget the whole deal. You're never going to make it in your own business. If petty details not only drive you to distraction but also keep you from working, then you won't do the job well. On the other hand, if you're a true self-starter—and don't even think of kidding yourself here—if you enjoy starting projects, both simple and complex, and bringing them to a clean close in good time and on budget, then you've got a great chance of setting up a successful carpentry business for yourself.

YOUR WORK WEEK

The old adage about working for yourself—I can pick any sixty hours out of the week and work that—is not really true. You've got to stay within the 9-to-5 world—6:30 to 4 when you're dealing with carpentry suppliers—of business. You will, however, find yourself working sixty hours and more many, many weeks, often back to back. This cubic increase in working hours may slacken as time passes and success jumps in your lap (you can afford to hire more help), but you almost never get a chance to work a forty-hour week when you're self-employed. You're either short of work and dreaming of working a full week, or you're working two-for-one. If you're succeeding, you will not be short of work with great frequency. The loss of spare time is one of the greatest sacrifices you will make in working for yourself if your business is to have any chance of success.

YOUR BUSINESS AS A PROJECT

You need to be organized, detail-oriented, and able to juggle several—often many—projects at the same time. The projects are not always going to be construction projects: Your business itself is a project, and the most important one. With no new business, no other projects get done, and you don't make a living.

One problem with moderate success in any small, home-based business is the temptation to do the work that's in and let the future worry about itself. I've done it; it cost me many, many months of time and a lot of money. You must balance working with marketing. You cannot put all your time into driving nails, sawing wood, and hanging Sheetrock. You absolutely must get the next job and the job after that in order to hold on to some of the profit from the job at hand. And to make that profit in the first place, you'll have to be a peerless estimator when bidding on a job. Having the greatest job sites, safest workers, finest designs, and best craftspeople doesn't mean a thing unless you make money on your jobs. If you don't make money, you won't stay in business. Money may not be your primary motivation, but it has to be a major prod or you'll never work as hard as you're going to need to work.

HONESTY

You'll notice that the questionnaire on the next page doesn't ask for your opinion about the need for honesty in business dealings. I'm assuming that anyone going into business in today's climate realizes that, outside of politics, honesty really is the best policy. Although it's a cliché, it happens to be true. Do good work. Do it when you say you will for the price you quote. That's honesty, and it brings repeat business. On the other hand, don't assume the other party in a deal is as honest as you are. Hope that person is, but do *not* assume it. Use a local credit investigation company, and create clear, and concise, contracts that bind the client to payment at specific steps (depending on job length, cost, and so on). Don't take a client's word for it that he or she has $75,000 to put into a large remodeling job unless you see some signs of major amounts of cash or the client has an excellent credit rating.

START-UP QUESTIONS FOR OPENING YOUR OWN HOME CARPENTRY BUSINESS

Possibly the most important qualifications for working out of your home are those that are almost totally unrelated to the business you start and run. For any small business to be successful, certain qualities are essential to the owner/operator. The following questions will help you determine whether or not you fit the mold.

1. Are you energetic?
2. Are you willing to work longer hours, and work harder, than you have ever done before?
3. Are you a self-starter?
4. Do you work well without someone telling you what to do next?
5. Do you work well under pressure?
6. Are you organized?
7. Are you a take-charge kind of person?
8. Are you well disciplined?
9. Will you make the sacrifices you must make to succeed?
10. Do you assume all your business dealings will be with honest people?
11. Will you do the scut work, the clean-up and set-up, without feeling angry?
12. Do you work best as a team member?
13. Do you procrastinate?
14. Do you think work must be fun?
15. Are you stern with people who owe you money?
16. Do you consider it necessary to meet or beat schedules?
17. Do you own sufficient carpentry or cabinetmaking tools and equipment?
18. Do you know as much about carpentry or cabinetmaking as you'll ever need to know?
19. Do you need a lot of people around?
20. Do you feel strict follow-up procedures are a waste of time?
21. Do you have to have peer recognition and approval?

You would be justified in wondering why you're not already in business for yourself if you answered "yes" to questions one through nine, "no" to ten, "yes" to eleven, "no" to twelve through fourteen, "yes" to fifteen through seventeen, and "no" to the rest.

WHERE TO BEGIN

You cannot begin without most of the needed working skills, even with helpers to fill the voids. It's too difficult to manage another person's work if you don't really know how that job is done. Small businesses require hands-on knowledge and lots of hands-on work. In the future, you may be able to skim the cream, but, first, you've got to learn to milk the cow, and that's hard work. Skills must be carefully learned while working for others. Skills must then be built up during your own start-up jobs; as you build those skills, you gather other needed items, including tools. Evaluate your skills in the area in which you intend to begin. If you're doing pick-up carpentry with no real specialization, make sure you have the skills needed for some fairly wide variations in job requirements. If you're doing remodeling, make sure your skills cover some of the wider and wilder requirements of that field. If you're doing custom building of residences, make sure you've got access to good plans sources, a good local architect, the best local warehouses, and building supply stores.

THREE DIRECTIONS

You can choose among three directions for your home-based carpentry business. You may opt for a basic carpentry business, doing any kind of wood framing and related work that is available, from extensions and remodeling to decks and additions. Many self-employed carpenters who begin by doing this kind of work then move into home building, a second direction, after gaining the needed experience. (Where I live, a number of the smaller building contractors also do wood framing when home building hits a slow stretch.) A third option for your carpentry business is cabinetry: You can make custom installations of already built cabinets or produce your own custom cabinets and install them in your customers' homes. The carpenter working in remodeling is going to be doing some, maybe even a lot of, cabinet installations, but a business that emphasizes this kind of work has certain advantages when trying to attract customers.

Select Your Type of Carpentry Business

This really is one of the first steps in a formal business plan: You must select the type, or types, of carpentry you plan to do. Hit or miss works fine for a time. You can make a decent living that way, taking anything that pops up. You may find yourself in over your head, however, both in knowledge and resources, if you haven't planned for larger jobs or complex smaller ones. While deck building is a good specialty, for example, the complexities of even the more elaborate deck designs are easily mastered. Building a deck one week and taking on a remodeling job the next may be more difficult than you think. Remodeling may present you with far more complex problems that have no cut- and-dried solutions, so you must improvise. To improvise you must have a very solid foundation in construction methods of all kinds, as well as a good relationship with the building codes department in your area. You sometimes *must* be able to explain to the inspector or his boss why your way works well, and keeps things at or above code intent.

GAINING SKILLS

Learning the skills you need is critical to success in your chosen area. Carpentry and cabinetmaking are skills taught both formally and informally in this country, but we have nothing approaching the apprenticeship system my old boss benefited from in Poland. Charlie was approaching age sixty-five when I, then an eighteen-year-old, took the job he was offering for $1.25 an hour. That was pretty good money at the time; the minimum wage was 75 cents an hour.

Our first chore was shingling a barn roof, and the first day remains a major marker in my memory. Like so many teenagers, I was sure I was immortal, and flat knew I could work any old man into the ground. Sure I could.

By the time we got the day's supply of shingles on the roof, I was ready to quit. Charlie wasn't even breathing hard, though he smoked heavily. He proceeded to pop a few chalk lines, hollering at me to hurry up and get my end down so he could snap the lines. Immortality retreats in the face of a 20-foot drop off a roof to someone like me, who was born scared of heights. I retain that fear to this day, and do as little high work as possible.

We got the lines snapped, and I was sure it was time for lunch, but it was about 8:15. By lunch time, I was dead, or so I dramatized. Charlie commented, "It gets better." He said that often, and also noted, "You will get better." He was right. I learned a lot as time passed, and I learned slowly and well when I listened. One of the curses of youth is an inability to listen for any length of time, though, so my carpentry education was spotty.

Working with Top Builders

If building is strong in your area, the best way to pick up needed skills is to work with the top builders in your area. Top builders aren't difficult to identify. Like Steve Arrington in Bedford, Virginia, top home-construction people have a reputation to uphold, and work hard at doing so. Often they are known for being slow as well as good. They do not easily adapt to new fangled ideas, but they do adapt to the better ideas. Steve is a case in point. He didn't like pneumatic nailers. They were a waste of time and money and didn't do as well as the good old hammer. One of his crews talked him into getting a pneumatic framing nailer, however, and for most jobs, he's delighted with it. It costs more than a hammer, to be sure, but it speeds framing work by hours in a moderate-size building, and eases the stresses on the carpenters using the tool. There's another local builder who refuses to allow any air tools on his jobs. This builder also has a bias against framing hammers and refuses to let his carpenters use anything over twenty ounces. His jobs always run a bit over budget, and the framing isn't as tight as it might be.

New Technology

New technology is not always the best way to go. It pays to stand back and consider how a new tool fits into the jobs you're doing before jumping up and buying one. Consider, for example, how many hammers you can buy for the cost of one framing nailer and a small compressor—whew! Let someone else, someone with more money or less sense, assume the risk of proving the worth of new tools. When you're convinced that the new technology is going to save you many, many dollars in labor and may also produce greater quality on the job, then buy. You can't compare the $700 cost of a nailer and compressor with the $30 price of a new framing hammer until you realize how much time the nailer and compressor will save, day after day after day for your $15-an-hour craftspeople. If the new tools save you only an hour a week, you'll earn back the cost in about a year. If it saves you two hours a week, you'll earn it back in half that time. Six months or less is a reasonable payback period for a nailer and compressor.

Be a bit skeptical of most new technology, whether for the office or for your fieldwork, but be open to proof. Some new tools have changed the face of the trade. For example, Steve Arrington and his crews do most cut-off work with a power miter saw, as do most carpentry crews today. This saw has effectively changed wood-frame construction forever, because all straight and many angled cuts are made at a single site, instead of on a sawhorse at the installation point. The pieces may then be assembled as required, and the cuts will almost certainly be dead square or dead-on the required angle.

How is this a radical change? Well, when I was a kid, the circular saw was just coming into use. It eased (by a factor of at least five) the effort a carpenter or helper had to put into making a cut, when compared with using a handsaw. Using a circular saw requires skill, though. A squared line had to be marked carefully, at the proper distance, for a clean, square cut. Today you can mark your work and plunk a miter saw onto it and get a clean, square or correctly angled cut. The only mark needed is the standard carpenter's arrow—no square line need be laid down. One step saved, less skill needed, and a square cut every time. The power miter saw is a mighty presence on most job sites today.

Thinking Is the Greatest Skill

Much changes, but much stays the same. While using the newest tools saves time on the job, the carpenter still has to know what goes where, and what cuts are needed to make the "whats" fit the "wheres." The physical skills needed today in carpentry are simpler than they used to be, but the mental skills required to produce a good house, cabinet installation, remodeling job, deck, addition, or other project remain as complex as ever. If you can't figure out how to approach a project properly, you can't do it properly. Nor can you tell anyone else how to do it, so you're going to lose money. Steve Arrington says all standard residential construction is simply based on the right angle. That's true as far as it goes. But you still must decide which part of that angle to use.

What we've got here is an Aristotelian notion of knowing yourself, and knowing your skills. Get those two ducks in a row, and you can almost certainly make a go of a home-based carpentry business.

Lead Versus Journey Level

Before you open your own business, try to get experience as a lead carpenter. A journey-level carpenter has all of the craft skills needed to make a success of the carpentry business but seldom has the experience of running a crew and estimating work, both of which are essential for your success as a businessperson. Lead carpenters are up on the most current methods and know how to keep crotchety and independent craftspeople from each other's throats on hot or nasty days. They also know the prices of most materials, allowing them to do the preliminary work for a job estimate. The overall boss will almost always be the one who determines final estimates and will also be the one who determines just what, and in what manner, a lead carpenter does. Some leads do nothing but direct the crew. Others get more responsibility. You need to aim for more responsibility: You'll have it *all* the day you open your office door.

PAYING TAXES

Dealing with the Internal Revenue Service (IRS) is one of the more frustrating tasks of running your own business. The IRS often seems specifically designed to drive the small businessperson completely insane. The easiest way to deal with that outfit is to keep detailed records of everything you buy that's deductible. And check with your accountant to see what is and isn't deductible: Your accountant needs to be prodded to give *you* and not the IRS the edge when a deduction seems debatable. If you've got a legitimate difference of opinion with the IRS, you'll have to pay back taxes, but there should be no fines or penalties. (There will be interest, though, at whatever the current rate is.) That said, it is also best to remember that the IRS is monolithic, answerable to no one, and can dog your tracks for life, making it fairly miserable. So make sure the deduction is worth it if you anticipate a fight. Keep track of every single *penny* of income. If you miss a deduction, you lose a few bucks. If you miss declaring income, you are breaking the law. Seek out professional advice if you have any questions.

INSURANCE

While some types of business can afford to skimp on insurance, carpentry isn't one of them. Skimping on liability, disability, and health insurance for yourself and the people you eventually hire is so risky as to be beyond sensible consideration. All your hired labor may be casual at the beginning and can be listed as independent contractors, but you still must provide liability coverage for the job as a whole. Talk with your insurance agent or broker, aiming at getting the best possible coverage in all areas for the lowest possible cost. It is still going to be expensive, but there are too many things that might happen on any job that can immediately cost you a fortune. And you will have to pay out of pocket if you're not insured. Insurance issues are detailed in chapter four.

FINANCIAL CONSIDERATIONS

You'll need to decide how large you plan to start. This will help you decide how much cash you need for start-up. Reality must be faced here. You will need to write out a business plan (see chapter six), decide how much of your current assets you are going to use to get things going, and then talk to your banker to see how much the bank will loan you. You may or may not have to modify your plans and start smaller. When you approach a bank, you'll need a résumé of your accomplishments to date, as well as a business plan.

With knowledge of your craft, regardless of your chosen specialty, and of your own strengths and limitations, you can turn the challenge of operating your own home-based business into a successful reality.

CHAPTER TWO

GETTING STARTED

THE HOME-BASED BUSINESS TREND INCREASES

More and more businesses today are based at home, thanks in large part to an electronic revolution. In fact, not since the European Hanseatic guilds of the early Middle Ages have we seen such strong home-based industry.

Small-scale carpentry, though, has for many years been a home-based business as often as not. My first employer ran his business from his home, using his dining-room table to do his accounting and general planning. Today, that's not feasible. The IRS isn't going to accept the locus of a business as the edge of your dining room, not if you expect to be able to deduct anything worthwhile in the way of business expenses. Electricity, heat, and office space are nondeductible items if you do not have a separate space for them.

MANY NEEDS TO BE MET

In spite of the IRS rules, many home-based businesses kick off each year, all of them helped by late-twentieth-century technology and some of them formed because of it. That technology can help a carpentry/cabinetmaking business stay alive and healthy, but it cannot do the running of the business for you.

We're talking here of a start-up business done on the proverbial shoestring. My assumption is that one or two people desire to start a business and are capable of hiring one or more helpers, as needed, to complete a job. For jobs requiring more people, remember that *you* can hire subcontractors as well as anyone else. In the meantime, get the office set up.

Setting up an office at home is a relatively simple job, especially if you figure no one is going to see it. Stick a desk in a corner; put a file cabinet and a plans bucket next to the desk and a trash basket on the other side. Plunk a phone onto the desktop, and start making calls.

Sometimes it's that simple.

But there are a few buts. First, you'll be driving a vehicle that may or may not fit into your neighborhood's overnight parking regulations.

Where I live, anything short of six Bradley fighting vehicles is unremarkable. In other, tonier suburban areas, simply parking a dirty pickup with ladder rack and ladders is enough to bring down the ire of the entire community. Given my temperament, I'd move out in about thirty seconds, but that isn't always an option. You'll need to check around and see if parking your pickup and other gear overnight might provoke your neighbors or cause you legal problems. Check it out first, and talk to those who might object the loudest.

You're probably not in a problem area, since working as a carpenter or cabinetmaker doesn't usually pay enough to allow you to live or loiter long in fancy subdivisions, but keep the thought in mind for later in life, too.

ZONING

Local regulations dictate the type of business, if any, that is allowable in a given neighborhood. Because you will be operating only an office, there should be no problem, but check first with the city or county clerk, or whoever you're directed to.

You may find your home office classed as a secondary use, and you may encounter some restrictions. For example, your business may be limited to no more than 25 or 30 percent of your home or an accessory building. Many communities still do not regulate home-based businesses, but trying to slip by without notifying local authorities can create later problems.

If you end up in court, you may hear references to "customary home occupations," which will include artists, writers, lawyers, doctors, music teachers, and many others. Nowhere have I found building or carpentry specifically included or excluded from this category. Cabinetmaking, which requires a wood shop on the premises, may well be prohibited—something to consider when selecting the type of carpentry you wish to pursue. The fact is, it is essential to check local regulations unless your next-door neighbor happens to be a carpenter and can answer all your questions.

Signs May Be Nixed

Even if no other prohibitions exist, you may find yourself prohibited from putting up a sign, or only able to put up a sign of certain dimensions and without lights. Generally, prohibitions against lights are not a problem: Garish, strongly lighted signs probably don't bring a builder much business.

You may also find that parking is limited. Most of us drive trucks, usually pickups, and we often have ladder racks. We are usually commercially licensed for insurance purposes, if not to satisfy the local laws. If we then add a sign, or several signs, to the truck, we may be eliminating any possibility of abiding by local parking regulations, even in our own driveways or in front of our houses.

If you can't park a truck with a sign, check to see whether you are allowed to park the vehicle without signs. If you feel truck signs are an essential part of your business, go to an office supply store and buy a strip-off sign. You can apply it in seconds, and it will come off just as quickly.

Limitations on the types of businesses allowed in the home usually have to do with noise levels and traffic. Most communities define home-business use as one that is an accessory use, thus either in an outbuilding, such as a garage, or in a minor percentage of the house. The percentage of the house used for business purposes is never to exceed 30 and often is limited to 20 percent.

Types of Home Businesses Classed As Customary

Doctors and lawyers fit the customary home-business category, as do artists, writers, and music and dance teachers. Architecture is also allowed.

Some city and town regulations defy reason. Chicago has an ordinance against the use of electronic equipment in the pursuit of business, which effectively outlaws word processing, accounting on computer, desktop publishing, and a host of other businesses.

Not far from where I live, Fairfax, Virginia, disallows antiques shops and funeral homes as customary home businesses, but specifically allows cabinetmaking shops. The first two are among the quietest businesses there are, though certainly many people feel uneasy living near a funeral home. Antiques shops, at least busy ones, can increase traffic in any area, but so does a cabinetmaking shop, and the cabinetry shop is also noisy. These examples illustrate the inconsistencies of home-based business laws. They also explain why so many people operate home-based businesses without notifying local authorities. Many artists, writers, architects, word processors, and others are simply setting up and going about their businesses without benefit of local legal blessing.

Local laws are often archaic. They limit such things as the use of outside help: In some areas, you and your family—even if there are a dozen of you—may operate a business in your home, but if you hire a single non-family member, you're in violation of the law and can be shut down.

Land Use Guidance Systems

Bedford County in Virginia has a land use guidance system (LUGS), once considered the up-and-coming way of dealing with land use problems without having real zoning regulations. Once a business has met specific neighborhood guidelines, LUGS allows the community to make the final decision. Unfortunately, a community can be pretty arbitrary about the businesses it refuses and accepts.

Preliminary Check for Problems

If you anticipate problems with zoning or other local regulations, investigate them in a low-key fashion. Check with various zoning and real estate offices as if you were in the very first stages of thinking about starting a business, no matter how close to setting up you actually are. You might start by saying, "I'm beginning to think of starting up a small building business, using my home for an office. I'd like to check and see how regulations affect that."

If there's any resistance, or if the zoning or LUGS regulations appear weighted too heavily against you, hire a local lawyer familiar with the laws and regulations. The investment in the attorney's time and effort will be worthwhile if you are saved the hassle of having your new business shut down because of a violation within a month (when you don't know, and can't find out, that such a regulation exists).

If your town's land use ordinances, whether standard zoning or LUGS, require that you follow formal procedures, starting with an application and a fee, and ending with a neighborhood meeting for approval, you can be sure you will need an attorney. He or she will make sure you don't miss an important step in the process that may later create problems.

There's no way to predict what kind of restrictions you might find in your neighborhood. Be sure to check them out.

Coming Changes

Many communities are now leaning toward land use guidance systems or similar land use procedures. They are helpful if applied fairly. The advantage of such a system for a home-based business is simple: If your business isn't going to disturb your neighbors, it's going to get a good, high rating, and acceptance will be almost certain.

Systems with land use classifications based on such observable criteria as potential neighborhood disturbances are probably best. If you don't make a mess, don't create masses of heavy traffic, and don't require special sewage lines (or septic treatment setups in rural areas), then there's a good chance your business is going to be acceptable under LUGS or similar regulations.

A home-based carpentry business should be looked upon favorably by the community because the noisy work is carried on in the field, and you seldom need more than one person in the office, particularly at the beginning. You will not add much to existing traffic, and usually won't have many vehicles parked in the neighborhood. Your sewage and electrical draws shouldn't be much higher than those of surrounding residences. You will not be putting out any more air pollution than anyone else who operates a vehicle.

TAXES

Tax regulations, local and other, can be a nuisance. Here, in Bedford, Virginia, I pay an annual property tax on office equipment, and if you think it doesn't annoy me (though it's seldom more than $40) then you think wrong. You start the process by paying for the property. At the same time, you pay sales tax on the property, but you've already paid income and other taxes on the money you use to buy it. Then, each and every year, you must pay a personal or business tax on your already taxed property.

It's up to you to check the need for applicable sales taxes on remodeling jobs and work on new homes. Allocation of sales-tax monies differs from area to area, with percentages specified for immediate localities ranging from tiny to huge. Such taxes are an inescapable drain on the wallet in most states today and will eventually reach all states. Even Nevada is thinking of getting into the act, now that most states are competing with them for gambling revenues.

You must check on sales-tax liabilities as well as on state and city income-tax liabilities. Such taxes are your responsibility, not anyone else's. See chapter three for further details on taxes.

LICENSES AS TAXATION

Calling a tax a license fee is a method of misclassifying taxes so that they don't seem quite as onerous. Fees for required licenses will vary from place to place. Some licenses are reasonable, such as tests that are given to determine the level of competence of a contractor, for instance, after which the contractor may qualify for a Class A, Class B, or Class C license. Such regulations reduce the number of fly-by-night outfits that hurt everyone's reputation.

Local regulations where I live require a false-name license. Your town, county, or other political district probably will, too. The cost here is only $10, and, in fact, the license is only required if you use a business name that doesn't include your personal name, though most banks insist on having a false-name license in hand before they'll open a business checking account for you. Banks are a little like governments. They make all sorts of regulations you cannot break—or the bank will either fine you or refuse to do business with you. As a builder, you *must* have banks, so you can't fight over unimportant things.

Various other licenses may be needed. Gross business receipts may be taxed. All of this must be checked before you open your doors.

Record Keeping

One tax liability that will create some immediate tax problems is the home office, if it is not impeccably set up. You need to save all receipts, and keep them for many years (seven is a minimum). You need also to make sure your office space, if it is to be deducted, is kept separate from the rest of the house. The IRS requires a door that can be closed, though in real life it may only be closed should the IRS auditor come to your home to check into the square footage of your office and other business deductions that you claim. That automatically knocks your 50-square-foot office into a corner if you plan to deduct any of the space.

I no longer bother. I currently have a closed-off space of more than 210 square feet and a storage building that is quite large, with the center third totally in use for business. I do not bother deducting the square footage of the space I use for my business because it is such a hassle to calculate proportions of this and that for a small percentage of actual space used in the house. I'm entitled to deduct a portion of my utility bills as well, but for the $250 or so it might save in taxes, it creates about $5,000 in aggravation because of the way the rules are written. I also don't recommend my way of doing this, because it can lose you some money each year. Eventually I'll change to full deductions as I increase the amount of space I use for business.

IRS Publications

Read all the IRS publications on home offices before you decide whether and how to make deductions. Call the IRS and request Publication 334, *Tax Guide for Small Business*; 505, *Tax Withholding and Estimated Tax*; 917, *Business Use of a Car*; and 525, *Taxable and Non-Taxable Income*.

It's a good idea to review all the forms and literature that the IRS has on small-business taxation. As a start, you're always going to need good old Form 1040. If you've ever been able to use one of the simpler versions, you can now forget it. You'll also have to have Schedule C, which covers profit or loss from business. Schedule SE becomes imperative, since you are now paying self-employment tax (with no employer to kick in half, the rate is double). You may need Form 2106 to record employee business expenses, and you'll certainly need 1040-ES for your own estimated income taxes. To deduct for costly tools and equipment, you need Form 4562, which has to do with depreciation and amortization. Currently there is also Form 8829, which covers expenses for the business use of your home.

You'll need more, but these forms and booklets will get you safely started. I'd suggest asking an IRS employee what else you might need, but every single time I've asked the IRS for information beyond their printed matter, the IRS has been wrong. Every time. The kicker here is the simple fact that wrong is wrong in the eyes of the IRS, so if you owe more because of an IRS employee's mistake, you still have to pay. I suggest you ask your accountant for his or her interpretation when you have questions. See chapter three for further details on taxes.

OFFICE EQUIPMENT

The basic office, as noted earlier, requires little more than a filing cabinet, trash basket, telephone, and plans bucket. A desk and chair are handy, but I know people who use drafting tables and stools. Your desires are paramount here, assuming costs are within your budget and you really can work out of such a setup. I place far greater importance on having a good electric drip coffeemaker, for example, than an attractive desk. Some use tables and chairs.

Whether your office is fancy or casual is up to you. What you need is a place that enables you to work efficiently. The home office is the foundation of the successful carpentry business you're attempting to set up. Efficiency is far more important than fanciness, but it's easier to operate out of an office that is at least modestly attractive. While you may have few customers filing through your office, especially in the early days, you have to spend considerable time there yourself. From hard experience I can promise you'll work better in an attractive, clean office. I'm terrible about office housekeeping—filing is my worst job—but I do keep the trash cans emptied and the floor swept.

Spend a little time and energy to arrange your office to suit you. You won't regret the extra time or the few extra dollars that an attractive office costs.

START-UP COST ESTIMATE

Getting started in a carpentry business doesn't take a huge amounts of money, but some equipment and supplies add to the basic start-up costs. Many carpenters go light on the fancier office equipment at the start. The list below provides for low, medium, and high estimates, and indicates cases in which equipment may be bought later, or lower-cost equipment (used or otherwise) may be bought now. For our purposes, start-up costs here do not include the needed six months' operating cash (including your salary) as described in the chapter on creating your business plan.

	Low	Estimate	Medium	Estimate	High	Estimate
Decorating and remodeling	None		Paint and clean-up, minor work		Complete re-do of area	
Furniture and fixtures	Used desk and chair		Used desk, chair, extra tables, chairs		New	
Office equipment	Used typewriter, answering machine, telephone		Used computer, answering machine/ telephone		New computer, fax/answering machine, typewriter	
Carpentry equipment	See list in this chapter for minimum		Mid-range, including heavier, more costly power tools		Everything on list, plus	
Vehicle	Used pick up, 2WD		Used pickup 4WD		New pickup	
Insurance	Essential		Essential		Essential	
Legal and professional fees	As required by locality		As required by locality		As required by locality	
Office supplies and materials	As required		As required		As required	
Stationery and business cards	Simple, low-cost paper		Fancier, higher cost, matching letterhead and business cards		Fancy envelopes, letterhead, business cards, labels	
Advertising	Yellow Pages		Yellow Pages, local paper		Yellow Pages, local paper	
Unexpected costs	Keep to a minimum with good planning		Keep to a minimum with good planning		Keep to a minimum with good planning	

USING A COMPUTER

Accounts are far more readily and easily kept on a desktop or portable computer than in a ledger book. For many good accounting programs, all you do is set up once, enter your material as desired, and get the reports you need to do taxes and figure investments.

After many years of using Moneycounts, I've begun using Quicken to do my books, and I'm finding it easy to use, except for some minor hassles. (If you can find a computer program other than a game that doesn't present at least minor hassles, drop me a note.) I dropped Moneycounts because I got tired of annual upgrades that added to program complexity without offering me any real benefits. I recently dropped Quicken and returned to Moneycounts. Financial reports are part of the everyday chore of doing business, and accurate records need to be kept to get accurate and useful reports. The computer makes keeping these records and generating the useful reports you get from them much easier.

You don't need to be a computer expert to use these tools. That's right, tools. A computer may be a bit more complex than your nail puller, but it's still nothing but a tool. And it really isn't all that complex. Computers are a pile of super-speed on-off switches. The complexity comes in arranging the switches, sticking that monitor (think of it as a small TV set) on top, and figuring out a way to arrange the data you put in the machine.

I will not recommend estimating programs because I don't believe one currently exists that will do a reliable job. Keep track of the programs in your trade publications, and you should have few problems settling on one, if you want to use a computer program.

Selecting a Computer

First off, I need to explain my biases: I don't use Apple computer products, though I have friends who do. I don't believe Apple's current products match PC-compatible computers for general business work, though for illustration and publication graphics they still retain a *very* slight edge. The business program edge held by the PC is much wider, and you will be working with business programs almost exclusively, so the Macintosh, including the Power Mac, is not a good buy. This is particularly true in light of current problems at Apple and the fact that Apple products invariably are more costly (at least 20 percent higher, often more) than various PC clones. Newer Apple machines may change all of that, but the basics have held true for upwards of fifteen years. Apple is easier to use, costs more, and does a bit less when it comes to business use.

Of course, if you get the hots for a fancy computer, you can slide five grand out of your wallet even for a PC, but such prices are for models better suited to much fancier things than keeping you organized and publicized: You may want graphics programs that show your clients what you propose doing for them, or design programs that help you and the client bypass possible misunderstandings. Computers to handle that kind of graphic detail require more memory and generally much greater hard disk and CPU (main-chip) capacity and speed, plus enhanced video options.

Computer Basics

For basic business work, today's entry-level computing machine has jumped a couple of grades and is now the Pentium 100. By the time this book reaches the market, the Pentium 120 or 133 will have taken its place. I'm currently using the 120, replacing a couple of older models, and it is downright speedy. The Pentium is the next-to-the-latest in a long line of central processing unit (CPU) microchips made by Intel (and, now, two or three other companies, including AMD and Cyrix). The Pentium chip, along with what's called a motherboard, is the brain of the computer. The motherboard holds the CPU chip and a slew of other chips, plus the random access memory and much else, and it is the unit into which accessory boards for other functions are plugged. All else is extension, though essential to giving the computer any utility.

The computer case contains the CPU, motherboard, power supply (converting 110 volts to lower-voltage DC), disk drives, a couple of light-emitting diodes, plus the accessory boards that plug into the motherboard and let you connect your keyboard, mouse, and monitor. In case you've never heard any computer talk, the keyboard is the part of the computer most like a typewriter. The monitor is the screen, basically a very high-definition TV set with the channel tuning guts pulled out (if you've got to have those soaps, you can spend a couple hundred bucks and add an accessory board that turns the monitor into a TV receiver). The mouse is another device that lets you put information into the computer; in computerese, it's an input device (like your keyboard).

Disk Drives

Disk drives are information storage devices. The main disk, similar in function to a massive file cabinet, is called a fixed, or hard, disk (also referred to as a hard disk drive or a hard drive). This hard disk is permanently mounted in the computer case and accepts a precise amount of data for storage. The ever-increasing storage capacity of hard disks in recent years has been startling. Capacities that seven or so years ago cost upwards of $10,000 are now selling for less than $300—and are far more reliable than the old models.

Floppy disks were for years the main method of transferring data from outside the computer to the computer's hard disk for use. Floppy disk drives come in two diameters, 3½ inches and 5¼ inches, and are mounted permanently in the case, but they *do not have disks in them* unless you specifically insert those disks. Floppy drives are used to install programs or transfer files to the hard disk, which then holds the programs and all files created by, or relating to, these programs.

The hard disk is the *big kahuna,* and needs special thought when you buy the computer. Look for something in the seek range of 10, 11, 12, or 13 milliseconds. (I'll be using some of these computer terms without explaining them, because only the dedicated computer nut is going to be interested in such explanations, and that person can readily find the details, or already has them.) Look for a hard disk with a capacity of at least one gigabyte. As a comparison, my first computer with a hard drive had a twenty-megabyte drive—a mere one-fiftieth of the capacity of a one-gigabyte drive. Unless you go nuts with graphics programs, a one-gigabyte drive will supply sufficient storage space for your entire computing career.

Other Drives

The CD–ROM drive is quickly replacing the floppy drive as the way to install information on the computer, and with its capacity of upwards of 600 megabytes, the CD–ROM also provides lots of removable library space, so it is possible to work all kinds of programs and activities that before took up space on your hard drive. A few years ago a single-speed CD–ROM drive cost upwards of a thousand bucks, and was slow as spit rolling down the outside of a window in a Minnesota winter. Today, you'll find sixteen-speed CD–ROM drives offered for under $200, and like hard drives, they're more reliable, faster, and cheaper than the drives they supplant.

A recent buy of mine is a thing called a ZIP drive, from Iomega. This is a $150 portable drive that also has a portable disk. (I got the portable drive because the fixed models had yet to come on the market in my locale, so you have a choice.) You can pop a 100-megabyte disk into the ZIP drive and work with the programs or material on it, and then transfer that disk and the portable ZIP drive to another computer to continue your work. You can also use the ZIP disks to back up the material on your hard disk, though at current prices that's a bit costly (disks run about $15 each, in lots of ten, but that price is going to come way down, if computer prices in general are any indication). The portable ZIP drive has become one of my favorite devices because it allows transfer of large files between fixed machines, portable comptuers, and all else. You can carry the lightweight drive with you, as you can the disks, and attach it to another PC in seconds and be up and running in seconds more.

Your Computer System

I suggest you buy a packaged computer system from a reputable vendor, either locally or by mail. If you are totally lacking in computer experience, you may be better off buying locally, although a friend of mine up in Boston bought his first PC by mail order from the manufacturer, and he is delighted with the entire setup.

Basics to buy: a mid-tower case; a Microsoft split keyboard (I'm using one, and it makes a tremendous difference in wrist and forearm comfort after a day or two of solid keyboard work); at least a one-gig hard drive; a 3½ inch floppy drive (the 5¼-inch floppy drives are virtually obsolete); eight-speed CD–ROM; a minimum of sixteen megabytes of 70-nanosecond or faster RAM; a 28.8 bps modem, and a decent monitor. Start with a Pentium 100, but check pricing on the 120, 133, and 166. There is a 200 version out now, but it is the super-costly, top-of-the-line, full-race model that very few users will ever need (including 97 percent of those who buy them out of perceived dire need). Depending on the monitor and extras chosen, this package is going to run well under $2,000 (with a 17-inch monitor, it should run about $2,700, and even less as time passes).

When selecting a computer package, you will get some installed programs, but probably not exactly what you want, and often they're not full-featured versions. One of the top word processors or word processing suites must be included, as must the Windows operating system. Windows 95 is rapidly becoming the new standard. Most newly developed programs will not operate on older versions of Windows, and DOS as a stand-alone operating system is just about dead.

Portable Computers

You don't need a portable computer, but will soon, or you'll believe you do. This is a field changing even more quickly than the basic desktop computer field, and it is one where specific recommendations are hard to make. Understand that you will pay more for less with the portable computer: You get less hard disk capacity, less memory, a slower CPU, a smaller and dimmer screen, and a keyboard that can give you carpal tunnel syndrome in about thirty minutes. For all of that, the field is growing, and people often pay well over five thousand bucks for these things. Forget it.

Do *not* try to make a portable your main computer system, and you'll be a lot better off. If you must have a portable, keep it modest. Go for a 486 CPU rather than the faster but more costly Pentium. Ask for sixteen megabytes of memory (regardless of what anyone says, the first versions of Microsoft's Windows 95 operating system do not work worth squat with less memory). Look for a 300- to 600-meg hard drive and a decent screen, plus some form of trackball to replace the mouse.

After that, it's all expense. Fancier screens are wildly expensive, as is a larger hard drive. You may find a Pentium 75 for about the same price as a slower 486 CPU, in which case, go for the Pentium. You should pay less than $2,000 for the package, but honestly, it isn't even worth paying even that much for a portable computer unless you're on the road and out of town an awful lot. Impressing people doesn't count here.

Modems

Adding a modem to your computer will let you do a lot of things, including dialing into the Internet—or as it is too often called, the information highway. There's a lot of good information on the Internet, but there is also a lot of nonsense. In fact, the ratio of time-wasting material to worthwhile info on any subject seems to be about 193 to 1. I'm connected to America Online and have also, from time to time, hooked up to Prodigy and Compuserve. Sometimes they're helpful; usually they're interesting. Microsoft runs a small-business center on America Online that is filled with interesting and useful information.

A modem is also handy for other uses. It can be one of the type that allows you to program voice mailboxes and similar features that give the impression you're operating a much larger company than is really the case. (The menu of selections—punch 1 if you want the boss, 2 if you want the vice president, or 3 if you want the secretary who gets the work done—can also lead customers into desiring to punch you, but that's another problem.) A modem opens up an incredible number of possibilities involving transfer of voice and data information. If you want the fancier aspects, consult a local computer seller. In my experience, you will not get much satisfaction from office supply stores and similar places that deal in computers as commodity sideline. Go for the company or person who sells and installs nothing but computers and related gear.

Keyboards and Mice

Check out some keyboards at an office-supply store or computer dealer to see what kind feels best to you. You'll be entering a lot of material with this device, so get one that's comfortable for you. If you don't go for the Microsoft split keyboard I recommended earlier, get a wrist support (to help prevent carpal tunnel syndrome) for both the keyboard and mouse.

Carry out the same testing in selecting a mouse. I don't note a lot of difference in mice in the mid-price range, so go with the one that feels best to you.

Monitors

You are going to be offered a 14-inch or 15-inch monitor (skimpy diagonal measurement, just like the one that applies to your TV set). But go instead for at least a 17-inch monitor with a sharpness of 1,024 lines, with a .28 pitch. I used to recommend starting with a 15-inch monitor, but

Windows 95 eats more of the screen than earlier Windows versions. If you can afford it, spring for the 20-inch or 21-inch monitor. The big buzzard about doubles the $700 or so that a good 17-inch monitor costs, but the relief it gives your eyes after a long day of crunching numbers or checking proposals is well worth it. The best bet is a 21-inch monitor with 1,280 lines, with a .28 or .26 pitch. Smaller pitches are acceptable as are more lines (up to 1600 is currently available, though costly), but larger pitches are best avoided in any of these monitor sizes.

The computer is a useful tool for modern business, and almost an essential one in figuring totals on estimates, assembling larger estimates into neat packages, and in almost any use where a typewriter and adding machine at one time served well enough. Local community colleges offer courses in basic microcomputer use and in the use of many of the more popular programs. Take a good look at local offerings. You save an amazing amount of time by having someone teach you shortcuts instead of trying to take a voyage of self-discovery (the time-consuming way I've done most of my computer learning).

Cellular Telephones

For decades, telephones and answering machines, and their problems, have been a major part of every carpenter's business. There is no substitute for a good telephone setup. Today's technology has brought a good addition—the cellular phone—which allows you to be reached no matter where you are (within reason).

There are a lot of good deals out there, and you will be able to get one, but don't believe the twenty-bucks-a-month nonsense. Read the fine print. You're liable to roaming charges, networking fees, and general long distance and service fees that mean you are not going to get by with even minimum use for less than $50 per month. Extensive use will rapidly quintuple that cost.

I'm not going to give much advice on buying a cell phone, because they're changing even faster than computers, with less likelihood the base unit is going to be a great deal down the road. I've got a friend who bought an $800 top-of-the-line unit a few years ago and remains totally satisfied with it as he roams the sands of Nevada and carts it with him to Florida, Arkansas, and elsewhere. Another friend got almost a freebie—the basic phone provided with activation—but then tossed in another thirty-five bucks to get some features he wanted. Do you need features? If so, pay the few extra dollars. Also, buy an extra battery (you'd never buy a cordless drill with only one battery, so don't get a portable phone, or computer, with just one).

Buy the lowest amount of cellular service you can get by with. Try the base minimum for a couple of months. You usually have to buy a year's activation, so make sure the company you select is going to let you roam the areas you always roam without coming upon blanks in service. It's a simple matter to upgrade from minimum service, but far less simple to downgrade if you don't like the company, the reception, or any other part of the deal. You can waste thousands of dollars in a single year by buying too much cellular service. Do a fair amount of checking of the available phones, too. There doesn't seem to be any reason to pay more than about $75 for a cellular phone.

For the carpenter/builder, a cellular phone is a necessity. It gives you freedom of movement you've never had before. You can be in instant touch with home base, or with any client who is near a phone, allowing super-quick resolution of problems, as well as acceptance of congratulations on a job well done.

Pagers

I won't wear one and wouldn't ask anyone else to wear one. That being said, pagers can be a relatively low-cost way to keep track of your crew members. Personally, I consider pagers nothing more than electronic leashes. Generally only lead carpenters or foremen need instant contact, so you may wish to check into low-end cellular service before messing with a pager, which requires the user to find a telephone to make any substantive response.

TOOLS FOR THE REAL WORK

I assume you know enough about tools to make your own selections as you work, gathering all those tools you expect you'll need and forgoing those you won't need with enough frequency to consider buying. Very few small builders need bother with scaffolding and similar working platforms, for example. It makes more sense financially to rent heavy-duty specialized tools, such as Ditch Witches, until your business requires that you buy something that costly. General carpentry tools are covered in the list on the following pages along with miscellaneous items such as extension cords. For some jobs, you may find a need for a generator, at least for a few days. If your need is short-term, this should be a rental item. The list does not include tools costing less than $10, such as utility knives, awls, center punches, and other small items that are essential to doing a good job.

Keep expensive, specialized purchases to an absolute minimum, though you shouldn't skimp on either quality or special features on the tools you need. Buy the best hammers, handsaws, and circular saws you can afford. Do the same with tool belts, pry bars, screwdrivers, planes, and drills. For twist drills, the new titanium-coated types are a marvel of durability for most carpentry jobs. Cobalt is too costly unless you're erecting stainless steel buildings.

You may or may not share my biases: I hate spade bits and prefer to use auger bits and twist drills when I can, though I quickly switch to spade bits when there's a chance the bit is going to be used in sections with nails or other embedded metal. I also like to clean my hammer face at least thrice daily, using 400-grit wet-and-dry paper.

Power Miter Saws

Larger power tools, such as miter saws, can be bought as needed, though I feel they're essential on today's construction jobs. You can buy a decent straight-chop miter saw for less than $200, but the top-of-the-line compound miter saws are going to cost twice that, and more. The choice is yours. Remember that you're not fooling with a circular saw here, and the unit is not easily adjusted back to square when knocked about too much. Factory repairs are costly as all get-out.

What do these saws do for the carpenter/builder? With proper set-up, power miter saws speed work and remove complexity from angle cuts—and from straight cuts. Much lumber doesn't make it to the job site with dead-square ends, so a power miter saw set up to handle the work can shave the end of every piece so that you work from a square starting point. Be sure to provide support for longer boards so they don't twist and lift the saw off the work table. Use a 2x12 base, with nailed-on supports for longer boards, and your work table can be as long as you are ever apt to need.

TOOLS FOR BUILDERS

Tool	Estimated Cost	Essential	Nice	Luxury	Rental	Have/ Need
Circular saw		X				
Reciprocating saw (essential for remodelers & cabinet installers)		X				
Power miter saw		X				
Air nailer			X			
Air compressor			X			
Ladder rack for pickup			X			
Pickup tool box		X				
Truck		X				
Computer			X			
Printer			X			
Ladder, 28'		X				
Ladder, 40'					X	
Stepladder, 6' (2)		X				
Stepladder, 8'				X		
Tool bag		X				
Bucket Boss		X				
Sawhorses (2)		X				
Pump jacks			X			
Calculator		X				
Folding rule		X				
Measuring tape, 10' or 12'			X			
Measuring tape, 25'			X			
Measuring tape, 33'		X				
Measuring tape, 50'			X			
Measuring tape, 100' (not normally needed for remodeling, cabinetry)		X				
Speed square		X				
Try square			X			
Combination square		X				
Drywall square (4')			X			
Miter box (even with power miter saw)		X				
Chalk line, 50'		X				
Hammer, 13-oz. (for cabinetry, molding)		X				
Hammer, 16-oz.		X				
Hammer, 20- or 22-oz.			X			
Hammer, 28 oz. (for framing)		X				
Sledge, 8-lb.		X				
Engineer's hammer, 42-oz.		X				

TOOLS FOR BUILDERS

Tool	Estimated Cost	Essential	Nice	Luxury	Rental	Have/ Need
Cordless drill (12-volt or higher)		X				
Extra battery pack			X			
Corded drill, ⅜" or ½"		X				
Hammer drill				X	X	
Drill bits, 15-bit set		X				
Long-shank drill bits, ⅜", ½", ⅝", ¾"			X			
Hole saw, 4" or 5"		X				
Hole saw set			X			
Table saw				X		
Radial-arm saw				X		
Handsaw, 10- or 12-pt.		X				
Handsaw, 8- or 10-pt.		X				
Ripsaw, 5-pt.			X			
Compass or keyhole saw		X				
Hacksaw			X			
Scroll saw			X			
Pry bar, 36" (especially for remodelers)		X				
Crowbar			X			
Nail puller			X			
Screwdrivers, 6-piece set		X				
Safety goggles, or face shield		X				
Dust & mist respirators, disposable		X				
Respirator mask			X			
Steel-toe shoes		X				
Shop vacuum			X			
Power plane				X		
Block plane		X				
Bench plane			X			
Laminate trimmer (essential for cabinetry)			X			
Biscuit joiner (essential for many types of cabinetry)			X			
Jigsaw (power)				X		
Belt sander			X			
Random-orbit sander			X			
Extension cords 50' (2, #12, with ground); others as needed		X				
Tool belt		X				
Gloves		X				

Cutting miters is far simpler with a power miter saw than with any other. You have no more difficulty lining up the cuts with a hand miter saw, or with a handsaw or circular saw, but you don't get the ease with the first two, nor the accuracy with the latter two, that a power miter saw gives. And it's much easier, with a power miter saw, to slice off less than a blade's width at a time, shaving the edge to "creep fit" parts, making sure everything comes out perfect.

For molding and bevel cuts, the compound miter saws are tops, and they also serve for the other angle cuts, too. Small compound miter saws do light work well, while the heavier-duty models take just about anything you care to throw at them, within their rated capacities.

Miter and compound miter saws, then, are strong assets when building. The larger or more complex a job is, the closer to essential these saws become to today's builder.

If the power miter saw changed the face of carpentry some years ago, today's crop of excellent compound miter saws is making an even more profound change. Although the saws cost a lot, they earn their way. A basic 8¼-inch or 8½-inch slide compound model costs about $400 (Freud, Craftsman, Ryobi), and the 12-inch DeWalt, Craftsman, Delta, and others run close to that. The 12-inch dual slide compound Makita costs about $850, but if you do lots of molding and non-simple rafters, the double compound feature along pays for itself almost instantly, as it does with the 10-inch double-compound Hitachi model.

Pneumatic Nailers

The pneumatic tool category is growing quickly, and now includes a full array of finish nailers as well as framing, concrete, roofing, and other nailers. Again, the original outfitting is not cheap, but the time saved more than makes up for cost, given a little time in business. Framing nailers, among others, are also easier on the old carpenter's weak point, the elbow, where tendinitis and other problems set in quickly.

You have an option on use of compressors. Paslode produces pneumatic nailers that require special power packs and chargers but no compressor and line. Companies like Campbell-Hausfield, Porter-Cable, Senco, Stanley-Bostich, Makita, Hitachi, and a host of others make units tied to a compressor by a hose, and they cost about $150 to $200 less than the Paslode units. Paslode also makes traditional pneumatic nailers.

If you're considering a compressor, select one of at least 1½ horsepower, with 2 horsepower preferred. Going beyond two horses usually means getting a fairly tippy three- to five-horse model. Do it if you have to. You may choose electric or gas models, but remember that horsepower ratings of the two are not directly comparable. Instead, compare cubic feet per minute at particular pressures (you'll want at least 3 cfm at 90 pounds per square inch to run a single nail gun, and upwards of 5 cfm to run two).

Cordless Drills

Compound miter saws and pneumatic nailers are the most popular of the new tools for putting up wood structures, with the possible exception of new versions of cordless drills. I easily remember many years ago getting my first cordless drill. By today's standards, it was close to worthless (and it wasn't really worth much by 1978 standards). Today, you can select up to 18 volts (DeWalt's monster); 14.4 volts is the coming standard, up from 12 volts. Barring major new battery developments, 14.4 volts is about the limit for tools that are going to be lifted and used on a daily basis; handling the 18-volt model makes it quickly obvious that it is bulkier and heavier than lower-powered drills. It also costs more.

Prices for 14.4-volt cordless drills have dropped considerably, and you can now get a double-battery setup with a one-hour chargers for well under $200. Twelve-volt drills, once the powerhouses of the cordless field, are available for between $100 and $165, and those prices should only evolve downward over time.

Equipping yourself is a simple matter. Staying equipped with accurate, working tools is another. Too many builders and carpenters do not care for their tools particularly well, and the overall cost over time is high.

Compound miter saws and similar costly tools are good examples of why it pays to take care of your tools: Losing the use of an $800 tool once on each job is costly, even if it can readily be repaired. Losing use of a tool because of carelessness or poor care—things that are avoided with seconds of thought or a few minutes work setting up, breaking down, or preparing to transport a tool—is downright stupid. All of us can plead guilty at one time or other to locking the blade down on a miter saw, wrapping the cord, tossing the saw on the pickup bed, and driving on down the road.

And then becoming angry when the saw loses its accuracy quickly. Another two minutes and a couple of one-dollar bungee cords can secure the saw so it is not knocked out of whack during transport. Also, that full-shouldered heave of the saw into the pickup bed may impress the younger members of your crew, but a gentle lift works better.

Organizer and Tote

I've been very happy with a contractor's attaché, or brief bag, from Duluth Trading. This is a heavy-duty canvas, leather, and solid brass multipocketed valise that looks like a huge purse. It is at least one-third larger than similar bags my friends have from other sources. It is also about as sturdy as such things get, and comes in a dark green. You can fit in just about everything from an InchMate calculator to legal pads to a 100-foot measuring tape and plenty of pens and pencils. The price is reasonable, and the quality is great.

Portable Products (Duluth Trading's supplier), has come out with a couple of new brief bags that are making quite a hit, with one model available now in most hardware stores and the other by mail order from Duluth. One is a price-conscious contractor's briefcase (bag) in brown duck and green canvas, at about $40. When you get more successful, you may want to consider either the heavy-duty valise described above or the builder's attache, which I do not have but want to get. This green canvas and burgundy leather device, half overnight bag and half briefcase, costs about $120 plus shipping and is well worth it. For information on Duluth Trading, see the list of sources at the back of the book.

CHAPTER THREE

GETTING YOUR FINANCIAL HOUSE IN ORDER

While you must have a bank account for your business, financial planning is much more than the simple process of opening that account and keeping track of the balance. Business plans require some details, even though the details are financial projections, but so do the everyday chores of posting receipts and bills. Keeping track of details keeps a business moving.

In the world of figures, don't leave out the human element. A large part of the success of many small businesses is often the relationship those businesses enjoy with their bankers.

CHOOSING A BANK

When choosing a bank, check peak, opening, and closing times. Banks located in downtown business areas usually close well before uptown and suburban branches, and may not be open in the evenings. After all, if 99.99 percent of their customers have left the area, there's not much reason to stay open. I got caught up in this problem years ago, when I used a bank in the Wall Street area, where I worked. I lived uptown, near Columbia, and had check-cashing problems galore.

Peak hours can also be a problem if at certain hours you cannot even get into the bank to transact business because of long lines. Other things to check when selecting a bank include the size of the required minimum deposit and the minimum balance for a checking account or business savings account to keep it performing at least cost and most profit to the business. The lowest figures possible are best here. Does the bank insist on the complete legal waiting period before making funds from a check available to your account? If so, keep looking. You want a bank that makes funds available as soon as funds are made available to it, or sooner.

Cashing Checks

How much difficulty will you have cashing a local check for about $100? What if you have a check for a similar amount drawn on an out-of-town bank? Does the bank cash third-party checks? How much are you going to get stung for a deposited check that bounces? My admittedly local research indicates there's about a $10 range in such charges, per check, even in my small town. Why does one bank charge $25 while another gets by with $15? I'm told some banks still charge less than $10 for the same service, and that overall there's a profit margin of almost 800 percent on this service.

What's in an ATM for You?

For immediate cash needs, does the bank charge for ATM use? Do they charge for withdrawals and not deposits, or for both? This is another area where profit margins are said by some to be nearly 900 percent! In a small town, I see absolutely no reason for using an ATM machine after you've been there for about six months. Cities are a different story. If you decide to use the ATM service, check to see how wide an area the bank and the ATM network serve. If you're going to eventually pay for depositing and withdrawing your money (and eventually all ATM transactions will be fee only), get the best and widest deal going.

What Kind of Checking Accounts Are Offered?

Does the bank offer economy checking accounts? Are fees figured on a minimum average balance or a minimum dollar balance? (The average balance account is better for you.) What is the monthly service charge for the basic checking account? What does each transaction cost, if anything? How much are the checks? (Remember, you can get your checks from a discount check-printing house.) Does the bank have overdraft checking, against which you can write checks for more money than you have in your account?

Check the bank's rates on various types of loans for preferred and regular customers. This may be where you'll eventually do the greatest amount of business, so make a careful check on all types of contractors' loans, construction loans, and the different kinds of mortgages available to your customers.

Bank Managers

How easy is the manager or assistant manager to talk to? You're going to need someone who listens to your plans and specific needs, and if the banker is a staid, hard-to-talk-to person, then you may wish to look farther. Bank managers have reasonably wide discretionary powers, such as deciding who does or does not get a loan.

What the Bank Needs from You

What you need to have in hand when you open an account depends on the form of your business and how long the bank has known you. If you have a partnership, the bank needs to see the partnership agreement as well as evidence of registration with the county clerk. If you've formed a corporation, the bank needs a corporate resolution, which is written on a form the bank can supply. It should be signed by an officer of the corporation and bear an impression of the corporate seal.

If, as is most likely going to happen, you operate a proprietorship as a single owner, you need to make sure you have your fictitious-name certificate or a copy on hand. You should also use some device or subhead under the name and address to identify this account as a business account. This is especially important if you have other accounts in the same bank.

A fictitious-name form is a local device designed to let local governments know if a business is running under a name other than the one found on the business owner's birth certificate. Pure and simple, it is a taxation device. Some noise is made about it being a control against fraudulent business practices, especially by contractors, but it almost never gets used for that purpose. You pay a one-time fee, and a low one at that, and the statement remains in force until rescinded.

HANDLING YOUR BANK ACCOUNT

Keeping tabs on your checking account is essential and can often mean the difference between making it and going broke. Fill checks out correctly, and enter them in your checkbook immediately, as soon as they are written. Balance your checkbook regularly, and reconcile it with your bank statement as soon after the statement arrives as possible. This chore may be aided by some of the computerized accounting programs that operate as checkbooks, though I don't like that feature too much. (I always seem to need a loose check when I'm away from the computer, which creates entry problems with some programs. And my laser printer makes printing single checks a real pain.)

Check with your bank for the time limit on notifying the bank of errors, so you have a solid time frame in which you must reconcile your account. Notify the bank manager immediately if you find a problem.

Keep blank checks in a safe, protected place, and if they're lost or stolen, notify the bank, and in the case of theft, the police. Destroy blank checks that aren't going to be used, such as those from a closed account.

Keeping Canceled Checks

Canceled checks also need protection and long-term storage. The absolute minimum business storage for records is seven years. I believe the IRS requires a three-year minimum unless fraud is involved, but it simply doesn't take up that much more room to store your records for an extra four years. My current pile goes back a decade.

Accepting Checks

Accepting checks from other people is a large part of any business, and there are procedures that will help prevent your getting stung.

1. If a check shows signs of having been altered, do *not* endorse it yourself. Your endorsement means you've guaranteed the check to all who hold it after you, and if it has been phonied up, you might face a legal problem.

2. Don't accept a check written in pencil.

3. Make sure the check is correctly filled out, with the full date and the amount written in numbers and words.

4. Don't take a check more than a month old unless you validate its status with the bank on which it was drawn.

5. For out-of-town checks, ask for identification from the person presenting the check, unless you already know that person well.

6. Take your time when accepting checks. Distractions create mistakes, and rushing increases the probability you'll miss something important.

7. Cash or deposit checks as soon as you can after receiving them. Most states allow you thirty full days for a check made out to you, and seven days for one endorsed over to you.

Bounced Checks

There are three primary reasons for a check to bounce. It may be forged—there may be no account in the name appearing on the check at the bank on which it is drawn. The account may be closed, or there may be insufficient funds in the account to cover the check.

If someone gives you a forged check, your first step on learning of the forgery is to notify your local police. The importance of this step cannot be overstated: For insurance purposes, it is essential to get the forgery on record. In addition, the police may already suspect someone of forgery in your area and could use your check to help shut the crook down. If the forged check is a U.S. government check, also notify the Treasury Department and the U.S. Secret Service.

If you get a check for which there is no account, it is possible someone has accidentally used a check on a closed account. If at all possible, call the person who provided you with the check. If within a reasonable time you cannot make contact or get no satisfaction, report the incident to the police as fraud.

For those checks that come back with Insufficient Funds marked on them, call or otherwise contact the person who gave you the check. If necessary, redeposit the check. If this doesn't get you your money, try to work out a solution with the check writer, or, if all else fails, look into a small-claims-court hearing.

Reconciling Your Checkbook and Bank Statement

Regular reconciliation of your checkbook and bank statements can keep small mistakes from becoming large problems. Compare the amounts written on your checks with those in the bank statement, and then check your recorded deposits for accuracy, number, and dates against your statement.

Use an adding machine or a calculator with a paper tape feed to calculate your balance: The tape makes it easier to go back and check for mistakes.

If you find an error, don't just double-check your arithmetic. Do the same for the bank's. Its computers, adding machines, tellers, and other personnel use lots of backup procedures, but recently a teller shorted my wife $50, so banks do make mistakes.

Finally, if you can't find the problem, go to the bank and ask them to help.

TAXES, TAXES, TAXES

Your finances and taxes can be managed with the help of a calculator or a computer—this includes job estimating, and posting receipts and bills. The aim is accuracy, but ease and efficiency are important.

At the start of your business, you may need only a calculator and a Dome book (or some less self-explanatory register) to keep records in, but eventually as your records become more complex, you're going to wish for other ways.

Regardless of the reason or rationale, today's bookkeeping needs are strict, and strictly a pain for those of us who do not care for working with columns of figures. I can remember many years ago discovering how much ease the calculator added to doing taxes. I still do taxes with a calculator, but I no longer use the palm-sized machine to do my books.

Taxes and Allowable Use

The allowable use of a vehicle and of other major tools in a business changes each year. The basis is frequently the same and the changes are in percentages, methods of deduction and amortization, and such, making old forms no longer useful, and new ones difficult to learn. In general, I've found it more practical to deduct the entire cost of a business vehicle over the allowable period of time at the fastest possible rate allowed. You also deduct each and every cent you put into that vehicle to keep it running and in good condition. Gas is deductible, as are tolls, car washes, oil, lubes, tires, and tune-ups. General maintenance all comes off your bill up front, *if* the vehicle is for the exclusive use of your business. Keep a log of mileage, where you go, and why, to augment any receipts. Currently, the IRS doesn't require detailed logs of travels for total-business-use vehicles, but that can change without warning, so take no chances. It's always best to check with a professional about the regulations.

Home-Office Deductions

What kind of test is the IRS apt to apply to business use of your home or a part of your home? This, too, varies from year to year and right now is being more strictly interpreted than in years past. Generally, any portion of your home that can be closed off and used exclusively for business on a regular basis is deductible according to its percentage of your total expense (including amortization of a portion of your mortgage, home-owner's insurance, real estate taxes, electric bill, and heating bill). Some types of expense for the home office are direct (100 percent) deductible, and others are indirect (corresponding to the percentage of home space used for the office: let's say 20 percent). As example, painting the office area, at $200, is a direct expense, while a mortgage interest of $2,000 a year allows a deduction of 20 percent of that, or $400. Unless you're separately

MILEAGE RECORD

<Organization>
<Address>
<City, State, Zip>
<Telephone>
<Fax>

[Name]

[Title]

[Telephone]

Date:

DATE	START	STOP	TOTAL MILES	GAS/ OIL($)	PARKING/ TOLLS($)	MISC. ($)
		Grand Totals	$	$	$	

Approved by: _____

metered, electricity follows the same rule, as does heat, some insurance, and repairs to the main parts of the house (roof, exterior siding, and painting the exterior). Before you dive into this morass, check with your accountant.

If it sounds confusing, that's for no other reason than because it is confusing.

Principal Place of Business

To add more confusion, in the past couple of years the IRS has started getting hard-nosed about interpreting the "principal place of business" rule. Basically, that rule states that you must operate primarily out of your home for it to be eligible for deduction as your place of business. If you don't do so, then the deductions may be disallowed. As far as builders go, most of the work is done on other sites, but most of the support work for the field work *must* be done in an enclosed space. You'd have the devil of a time trying to keep records in the front seat of your pickup or in a living room that has yet to be roofed or show prospective customers plans in the mud of a wet job site. You need an office, and you save money and deductions (which should please the IRS) by placing that office in your home. The fact that you spend thirty-five hours a week at various job sites and only about fifteen to twenty hours in the home office should not be a problem.

Whatever you do financially, you must keep records, and those records must be detailed. There's a fine line between so much detail it eats away too much of your time, and enough detail to satisfy the IRS, should you ever be involved with an audit. No one ever writes of an audit by state agencies, though those do occur: In general, if the IRS audits you, you increase the odds of state revenue officials trying to do the same, but unless you are amazingly careless or fraudulent on a daily basis, state agencies seldom get into the act.

Keeping track of the IRS's rules is difficult, but there are various magazines that do the job, including many of the trade magazines for builders. In addition, *Home Office Computing* is a big help. Generally, *HOC*'s articles are geared towards businesses that combine graphics and desktop publishing, but the magazine covers programs and computer equipment of interest to a wide range of businesses. They use less jargon than most, too. For current subscription prices, call (800) 288–7812 or write *Home*

Office Computing, P. O. Box 2511, Boulder, CO 80302. The magazine comes out monthly.

BILLING

Billing on time, with details of what is being billed and what payment is due when, is a part of any business, and it can't be ignored if the business is to succeed. Much carpentry work is arranged for with a down payment. The remaining payments are due as work is completed or material is delivered (such as cabinets and other costly items). Your state may limit the amount of the down payment. Do not overload the front end: I know a lot of builders favor this device, but no customer I've ever talked to likes to lay out 90 percent of the cost of a completed building that is just then having the roof trusses installed. And I can't blame them.

A simple letterhead invoice is usually the best, with details of the work done and materials supplied all listed. The total amount billed is listed and a payment due date is assigned. The timing and specifics of your billing procedures will depend on the wording of your contracts. Contracts are essential to a well-run carpentry business, and as I get older I believe contracts, no matter how simple, are essential to the health of any small business.

TYPES OF CARPENTRY CONTRACTS

Like all such quasi-legal matters, contracts require the attention of a lawyer, at least at the outset of your business. The *whereas* and *whereat* parts presumably cannot be properly written without an attorney in attendance, and considering the complexity of some of the contracts I've recently read, it's easy to see why.

There are essentially three types of contracts that are useful to the small builder or anyone operating a home-based carpentry business: small job contracts, lump-sum contracts, and time-and-materials contracts. The basics of any contract, regardless of the type, are simple: The contract specifies in writing what is to be built, what it is to cost, and under what conditions. Writing a basic contract, whether it's created by you (not a good idea) or your lawyer, is a tedious job. Once it's done,

Getting Your Financial House in Order

though, you will need only minor or boilerplate changes (cost, date of completion, name of client, description of job, type of payment).

Small Job Contracts

Small jobs require very simple contracts. You specify what's to be built, include your estimate, divide the cost into three parts, and state three payment dates (related to completion). (For really small jobs, there may only be a need for two payments.) It simplifies your financial life if you get a check for half the total estimated cost up front, even on jobs that don't cost more than $1,500. Construction quality specifications are usually based on accepted industry standards, and, of course, on building a job that meets all local codes, regardless of what that job is. (Around here, if you're building something for agricultural use, you don't have to worry about permits or inspections, but it still makes sense to build to accepted standards.)

Large Job Contracts

The sort of contract you'll want for a larger job depends on your confidence in your estimating abilities and also on the type and quality of local competition. Two contract types exist. One, the lump sum, is very much like the small job contract, but larger in scope and scale. The time-and-materials contract has been modified in recent years and is now a cost-plus-fixed-fee contract, with the cost variable but the fee for the builder fixed at a specific percentage of that cost. In a really tight market, the builder's fee is a specific amount of money. The fee covers both profit and overhead, so the percentage basis is best for the builder, making sure there's a reasonable profit in each job.

High costs resulting from job-site difficulties not attributable to the builder become losses if he or she uses contracts with set amounts, including the lump-sum contract.

Both lump-sum and time-and-materials contracts can be abused by builder or customer. A builder may inflate his fee or do less work for the same fee. Or the buyer may constantly be in the builder's hair, switching walls from one spot to another and bathrooms from one plumbing stack to another. He or she may expect to pay no more than minor materials charges for the extra work.

Lump-Sum Contracts

If your estimating skills are excellent and you've got good, clear plans and specs, then the lump-sum contract is probably the best chance you have at making extra money. You'll need good weather-prediction skills when the job has much outdoor work and good market-prediction skills when wood and other building materials costs are on the upward run of the roller coaster, as they have been for the past year or two. Of course, to make money as a home-based carpenter or builder, you've got to have excellent estimating skills, anyway.

Lump-sum contracts generally are simpler and more cut-and-dried than time-and-materials contracts, with fixed payments set by contract and billed accordingly. This means you don't have to add up each bit of labor and material every ten days or so, as you do with the time-and-materials (T-and-M) contracts.

Basically, a lump-sum contract is clear and simple. If you made a high estimate, though still low enough to get the job, and come in on schedule, you'll nibble high on the hog. If your estimate missed, you're not going to eat so well. The customer takes no risk. The price agreed is the price agreed, and cannot be raised.

Time-and-Materials Contracts

For some jobs, the client must share the risk because there's no way you can estimate accurately the number of hours, the amount of materials, or even the quality of the materials a job might require. This happens most often in remodeling old homes, where you don't even know what's involved until you've begun ripping out walls. Severe deterioration is one problem you might face, and you may also run into old houses that bear so little relation to any known building specification or code, there's no way to accurately estimate remodeling needs. Around here, we've got a fair number of clapboard-covered houses that began life seventy-five or one hundred years ago as log cabins. In the ensuing years, additions in various frame styles were added. Opening up a room or changing a floor plan in one of the houses is a major adventure in discovering what beam or joist is apt to collapse next.

I well remember one house where I intended to do some underfloor insulating, using a stone crawl space (already not the ideal solution in this part of the country, because rock foundations are breeding grounds for copperheads—not my favorite slithery things). By the time I got underneath, I discovered the house did not have cut framing for the floors. The joists, sill boards, and all other floor framing members were unstripped white oak logs! The floor was insulated in late fall, when the air was delightfully far too cold for copperheads. Cutting batt insulation to fit on-center spaces that ranged from 12 to 36 inches and ranged considerably in a single span because of the taper of the logs was quite interesting. Fortunately, the big loss was my labor. A half-day job took three days. A T-and-M contract would have made me a few more bucks.

If you cannot accurately estimate a fairly straightforward job, you should probably not bid on it, but if you do bid, use a T-and-M. If your estimates are too far off, however, and you add many extra charges, you'll end up creating bad feelings. These bad feelings affect your best form of advertising, word of mouth.

On straightforward projects when you must begin work before the architectural plans are ready and you can't really firm up a price, use a T-and-M contract. This situation is much like the previously described remodeling and reconstruction jobs, when you cannot sensibly tell what's required until you start to peel the old house.

CONTRACT TERMS

A contract needs to treat all parties fairly. In doing so, it also needs to protect the builder or carpenter from conditions beyond his or her control, including the caprices of the buyer and possibly the architect.

You need to specify things not included in the estimates, such as building permits, any fixtures the customer has already bought, and in remodeling jobs, asbestos removal. If one of your subcontractors is doing work that requires the customer to select specific materials, you may wish to specify how that is to be handled. Let's assume you've got a plumber who is going to set a Jacuzzi, but neither you nor the plumber knows the model, and up until the last moment, neither does the customer. In such cases, have the customer work through the sub, with the sub buying the Jacuzzi and billing it to the customer for cost plus 15 percent. You may wish to follow the same procedure for ceramic tile, cabinetry, and countertops.

You must use a lawyer to get a reasonable basic contract that will cover different types of work, and I'd suggest getting one drawn up for each different type of payment, including two versions of the contract, one for smaller jobs without some of the complexities involving subcontractors. Ask around among builders for the names of lawyers who do good work for contractors, builders, and carpenters. See if you can talk a local builder or two—successful, nonblowhard types—into letting you borrow and look over copies of their contracts.

Then work out the fairest contract you can for your own work. It should be fair to you and to your customer, while also making sure that unforeseen slip-ups beyond your control don't become your fault. You must state in the contract, for example, that the customer will wear appropriate safety equipment (hard hat, goggles) while on the job site. Selections of all fixtures, cabinets, and similar items need to be made before the work begins, or long delays can develop as minds are changed and changed again. The customer must be limited in any work he or she might perform or subcontract for without going through you as prime contractor. Make sure any owner-done or owner-subcontracted work is completed before your work begins or after you're finished and off the site. Otherwise, you'll have delays. You need a solid legal description of the work site, including a survey if it involves any work such as pouring foundations or breaking ground; location of underground or other hidden utility lines; and soil reports. You also need to know the customer has legal title to the land you're building on.

For remodeling jobs especially, a contractual statement giving you free access to the job site is essential, and the contract should also specify that the customer move any and all property out of the area being remodeled. You can move the stuff yourself, of course, but if there's any problem, you get blamed for breakage. The customer must be obligated to keep children and pets away from the work site.

Decisions required from the customer as the job progresses must be made speedily, and the contract must specify compensation to you for any failure to make prompt decisions when that failure causes delays in the job.

CHANGES IN THE WORK

This is a spot where major problems may occur, and it is an area that can cause you to lose money faster than any other, except a lack of skill in estimating. In general, a customer has a right to order changes in any work you're doing, but only within specified parameters. Basically, owners do have the right to add, delete, or otherwise modify any project. That is a contract condition that almost always has to be included.

Other change orders come when job-site work reveals specific problems not evident on the surface, creating a need for additional work, more and different materials, and other problems. Too often, the customer thinks this sort of thing is covered without additional charge, so the contract must specifically state that the customer bears financial responsibility for such work. I suggest you specify at least the following items:

1. Subsurface soil conditions that require extraordinary methods of excavation, unless those methods are already specified in the contract.

2. Substandard framing, from out-of-plumb walls to out-of-level ceilings and floors. This includes much older work done with rough lumber or full or partial logs.

3. Asbestos that requires removal. This needs to be done by specially trained and equipped people.

4. Extra work in tearing down or installing anything because of subsurface conditions, such as wire in plaster, hidden insect damage, hidden rot, hidden heating, air conditioning, and other ducts, and hidden wiring and plumbing. I've seen houses where walls contained hidden fireplaces that were covered over and lost to view.

You also need to make sure the customer understands that natural disasters are not your responsibility, beyond normal protection against the elements.

There are a number of other areas to be covered, so make sure your lawyer is well versed in the legal needs of small building construction.

CHAPTER FOUR

INSURANCE

H ere is your introduction to the world of insurance. Insurance is essential because if things go wrong and you're uninsured, you no longer have a reason to operate a business, for you'll have no money to operate it with.

LIABILITY INSURANCE

General liability coverage on the job site and for later problems that could develop when the job is complete is one of the most important types of insurance coverage any carpentry business can have. You *must* have the guidance of a good agent or broker when drawing up your liability insurance plan, and the agent or broker can guide you to other types of insurance for the small business owner. My recommendations are general; there is a great deal of variation from state to state.

Insurance is not only super-important to the small carpentry shop—even if you are and plan to remain a one-person shop, you need lots of insurance—it unfortunately tends to be the largest single expense in the business.

Any tradesperson is best insured with a safe job site, the details of which will not be extensively covered in this book: If you're a good enough carpenter to think about starting your own carpentry business, you're good enough to keep a clean job site with safe conditions. But even safe job sites sometimes have problems; collapses and injuries do occur. These problems can be ruinous if you're not insured. Spreading the risk through insurance is essential. Plan carefully to get the best available insurance for the best available price.

At the outset, you must have liability insurance. Determining the amount needed is a personal decision, which depends on what you feel you have, or may soon have, at risk. Contractor's or builder's liability comes in many forms, with many arms: medical coverage liability for premises, damage to property liability, contractor's general protective liability, personal injury liability, fire liability, collapse caused by excavation liability, damage to underground utilities liability, and failure to build to specs liability. Generally, you want the kind of policy that doesn't specifically exclude much and doesn't exclude *unless* the exclusion is specifically stated. A long, long talk, or even several long talks with a very good agent is an essential ingredient of success.

When deciding the amount of coverage, you must consider the high costs of legal help when settling claims is required.

We all like to think we're the best and problems aren't going to occur, but of course they do. Let's suppose you're doing your first job—a remodeling job on a moderate-sized house. Your helpers are inept at bracing for wall removal, and the result is a collapsed wall on the house, which also brings down a bathroom with an occupant inside! The occupant is not permanently damaged, but suffers a few broken bones. The result is clearly your fault. The court or jury will find against you if the insurance company lets the case go to court. Bet on a settlement, however, with lawyers taking a fair chunk of the award to the victim.

Recently, my home area has seen a lawsuit from a person who dove into the shallow end of a swimming pool and permanently damaged himself. He is suing his pal, the pool owner; the national association for pool manufacturers; the pool manufacturer; and the pool installer—for a grand total of 20 million bucks. Why? This home pool had no DO NOT DIVE sign at the shallow end!

Now, not being a lawyer, I say the guy hasn't got a case. I've swum in dozens, maybe hundreds, of home swimming pools, and not one has ever had such a sign. I have never seen such a sign outside of rocky areas at some public beaches or in public pools. Nor is it particularly needed when, as in this case, there's a diving board on the opposite end of the pool, and an adult ought to know that home pools have shallow ends opposite their deep ends.

But lawyers are a different breed, and one saw a case here. I have no idea what the resolution will be, but the case was not thrown out of court immediately, as some of us had expected. While I sympathize with someone who is paralyzed, I don't think he should punish others for his own mistake. We live in a litigious world, though, so give some thought to just what making a mistake that creates property damage and injury can do to your business.

Umbrella policies are also available, and may serve to raise up your limits considerably at relatively low cost. A great deal depends on the way the umbrella is structured. It is essential to cover these policies, too, with your agent.

AUTOMOBILE INSURANCE

You will need business auto insurance because if your agent discovers you're using that old pickup for work, he'll be forced to cancel your family policy coverage. Check the various classifications to make sure you can get into the lowest priced one possible. The usual categories are commercial, retail, and service; rates vary considerably. Also aim at getting coverage for nonowned vehicles if you have any helpers who might be running errands in their own vehicles. This does not cover the driver of said vehicle: It covers you against problems arising should that driver be in an accident while on your business.

EQUIPMENT THEFT

This is a great coverage to have if you can get it at reasonable cost. It basically covers you against quick theft from vehicles and equipment at the job site. See if you can locate a policy that pays replacement value rather than cost, though to be honest, tools today do not seem to be increasing in cost as fast as the rest of our expenses. They're expensive, but not nearly as expensive as such items as insurance, building materials, and good quality labor.

WORKERS' COMPENSATION

Workers' compensation insurance provides financial support for injured workers, no matter who was at fault when the injury occurred. As an employer, you must, by law, provide medical care, compensation for lost wages, and rehabilitation for any worker injured on any of your projects. Most years, with good luck, good safety practices, and good workers, this probably isn't going to amount to more than a few twists, turns, cuts, and sprains. When more serious injuries occur, costs add up quickly and considerably. You can think of self-insuring, but let me assure you it is not sensible, practical, or, in many states, legal. Some states provide mandatory workers' comp, while in other states you have to go to private insurers. Some states let you do either.

Workers' comp may cost as much as 20 percent of salaries or more. Medical and rehabilitation costs add to prices, as does general inflation. The biggest factors, however, seem to be unsafe job sites and workers who are willing to sue the boss. You can help reduce costs by keeping your job sites safe and quickly treating all workers who are hurt, no matter how small the injury. Where possible, shop around for policies, too. Some trades are not as expensive to insure as others, so you may be able to re-rate one or two of your employees.

Safe work sites are important because they become a part of your overall record as a contractor, and there is usually a modifier for workers' comp based on past claims. Sometimes an insurance company will pay dividends when no claims have been filed over a period of time. Thus, a safe work site and a good safety record help stabilize and even reduce costs. A lousy safety record will cause premiums to rise, often very high.

Keeping a safe work site has advantages other than saving you money on insurance costs. Your workers are going to be happier if on-the-job injuries are few and far between, even though they must put forth a bit more effort to keep the job site clean and safe. In general, safe work sites make for faster completion of jobs—you don't lose time waiting for cuts to be cleaned and dressed or ambulances to transport workers to the hospital. You also don't lose time filling out insurance claims forms.

CHAPTER FIVE

MARKETING

arketing is nothing more than spreading the word that you're in the carpentry business and good at what you do. Marketing is especially important at the start-up of your business, but a continuous marketing program is even better. It's often possible to get free space and attention in local newspapers and in the trade press, but, just as often, you must buy some advertising space.

Word-of-mouth advertising works well for many builders, and this kind of unpaid advertising is probably the best there is. Local builder Steve Arrington just lists himself in the local, white-pages telephone directory and doesn't even take out a small ad in the Yellow Pages. He simply includes the abbreviation *bldr.* after his name. The last time I talked to Steve, he was booked up for upwards of a year. The Yellow Pages remain a good place to get your name out, though, and to let prospective customers know of your specialties, if any. In fact, if you weigh cost against results, your ad is probably going to do better in the Yellow Pages than anywhere else. That's not to say you don't need to advertise elsewhere. The frequency and placement of your advertising is a judgment that you must make over time. Right after you get a simple letterhead, some envelopes, and some business cards printed up, your Yellow Pages ad should come next.

As you can afford it, join the local chamber of commerce, Lions, and Kiwanis clubs, and similar social and business organizations. You benefit your community while also making invaluable contacts for furthering your business.

BUILDING A PORTFOLIO

Build your portfolio just as an artist, photographer, or writer builds a portfolio. You are a craftsman or craftswoman and have a right to take pride in your artistry. Make sure you have the right! Take photos of your work as you go along, particularly of difficult, unusual, or unique aspects of the job, and, of course, of the completed work. You're not going to be able to send prospective clients to each and every completed job to check your work, so good color prints are great as stand-ins for the real thing.

Your portfolio can be enclosed in plastic pages for protection: I suggest getting prints at least 5 x 7 inches in size, and 8 x 10 inches is even better. This does two things: Large prints allow the prospective client to see more detail and also look more professional. Twentieth-Century Photo Products and Accessories (call 800–767–0777 for a catalog) sells photo pages in minimum quantities of fifty. The pages accept both 5 x 7-inch and 8 x 10-inch photos. The company offers a low price on a three-ring binder with each fifty pages.

With an ad in the Yellow Pages, your white pages listing, and the right stationery, you're ready to start a small publicity campaign.

You'll note throughout I say nothing about electronic media. That's not a bias: I simply do not see what TV or radio does for small contractors. It works well for siding contractors who subcontract out to many subcontractors, and it works well for larger commercial construction contractors, but for the remodeler, home builder, and the cabinetmaker, I see little need to advertise on radio or TV.

WRITING A PRESS RELEASE

There are a number of things to remember when writing press releases:

1. Short is better than long.

2. Send the release to the business editor of your local newspaper or newspapers. (Call the editorial office and ask for the editor's name.)

3. Make sure there are no misspellings of important material.

4. Provide a call-back name and number. (Your own will do fine.)

5. Don't inundate the editor with material every time you have what seems a profitable idea.

6. The release must be typewritten, and it must be neatly done, with no cross-outs or visible correcting fluid used. If you can't do this yourself, get a friend with a computer and a word-processing program to do the release for you.

You want to announce that you're starting your business and, at the same time, list any specialties. Your next release might be six months later, on completion of your largest job to date, giving a short history of your company, and its major accomplishments. If you specialize in remodeling kitchens, state that as an accomplishment. If you've put in a kitchen in collaboration with an award-winning designer or architect, state that.

For your first release, consider following the form on page 56. Use it for your own press release, but change the content to fit your company. If you're forming a partnership, say so. If it's a Subchapter S corporation, that may be of interest to some, though probably not. You may wish to provide a more complete list of your services and skills: The provided sample is only a suggestion. Note that it is fewer than 130 words, which is a good goal, though up to 200 is permissible. Your aim is for your news release to be read and published. If it's two or three pages long, you're less likely to succeed. Editors are busy, and don't like to read a lot of extraneous material that they'd also only have to cut.

A second type of news release announces the awarding of a contract for a major job or the completion of a job that is, in some way, important enough to interest your local newspaper. For small contractors, it's difficult as blazes to determine what is offbeat or strong enough to get mentioned. One thing is certain, if you're completing a small job weekly, do *not* announce each and every completion to the newspaper. It won't print your release, but someone there just might associate your name with a lot of uninteresting junk—and there's a great deal of that coming in to newspapers from professional public relations outfits. So, don't send too many releases. No small company is going to generate a lot of earth-shattering

```
NEWS RELEASE
NEWS RELEASE
NEWS RELEASE
```

Contact: Jan X
Telephone Number: (703) 555-1212
Address: 999 Nutley Drive, Anytown

ANYTOWN, Any State, October 9, 1999—Jan X today announced the formation of Cabinetry Unlimited, a proprietorship that offers remodeling through custom cabinetry in old and new homes. The company goal is to provide increased storage, beauty, and general enjoyment of family living areas, using a variety of custom cabinets, in conjunction with other forms of remodeling, so that clients attain an unusual, often unique appearance and use flow with more moderate costs.

"Cabinetry Unlimited," said Ms. X, "will provide a wide spectrum of services for those who wish to get the greatest effect from their remodeling, without spending sums of money that might startle the Pentagon." Preliminary consultations are free.

Cabinetry Unlimited, or CU, is a fully licensed, bondable remodeling contractor and is located at 999 Nutley Drive, Anytown. The phone number is (703) 555-1212.

business news—most won't even make the grass wave more than once every couple of months.

But when you do deserve a release, get one out quickly. If you get an award for design excellence, superb craftsmanship, or something else in July, don't wait until August or September to write the release.

If you don't feel competent to write a press release, don't feel shy about checking out local freelancers to see if there's someone familiar with the construction industry who will write one for a reasonably modest fee. (Try to pay by check to keep the IRS off both your backs.) Newspapers are good places to check for names of freelancers, but you may want to get recommendations from editors of building and construction trade newspapers and magazines: Their freelancers are often ready and willing to do the work for little more than an inexperienced, local writer. There's no need for you to meet the writer, or, for that matter, for the writer to be near you and your business. Fax machines transfer finished work instantly and they're cheap to use. It costs me about 26 cents to send three pages about 900 miles. A three-page letter costs 32 cents for the stamp and that destination 900 miles away may take as many as four days to reach.

These three examples should simplify your relations with local newspapers and association and trade publications. Trade pubs aren't often a great deal of help unless you hope to do a lot of subcontracting. The reason is simple: The audience is made up of other builders. Association publications probably have the same drawback.

Marketing is not just a few small ads and simple news releases to local publications. Your best marketing tool is your own work, cheerfully done on time and within its budget. After that, work to let people know what you can do and how well you do it. Of course, you first must do the work before you get bragger's rights to the work's quality.

Your news releases may hit the buttons needed to get a reporter to talk to you about you and your business. And they may not. You may need

---

AWARD

ANYTOWN, Any State—XYZ Company today received an award for most creative use of two-by-fours on a drywall surface, using nailheads as decorative studs. The award is from the State Association of Bonded and Insured Building Contractors. XYZ Company was formed by Jim Jackson in 1994 as a home remdoeling business. Its goal is to create the kind of living space that appeals to people with growing families and parents whose children have already left the nest. Greater use of limited space is one feature of XYZ Company work, while more openess in living styles is another.

This is XYZ Company's third award for quality or creativity since the company was founded just two years ago. The company is a fully insured, licensed remodeling contractor for Any State.

XYZ Company is located at Bumblebee Drive, Anytown. The phone number is (703) 555-5555.

LARGE CONTRACT

ANYTOWN, Any State—Jim Jackson of XYZ Company today announced the awarding of a major contract to install residential greenhouse subsystems in homes built by American Homebuilder Corporation. XYZ Company was formed by Jim Jackson in 1994 as a home contracting business, with a goal of creating the kind of living space wanted by people with growing families and by people with families that have already left the nest. Greater use of limited space is one feature of XYZ Company work, while more openess in living styles is another.

This is XYZ Company;'s largest contract since the company was founded just two years ago.

The company is a fully insured, licensed contractor for the state of Any State.

XYZ Company is located at Bumblebee Drive, Anytown, and the phone number is (703) 555–5555.

HIRING

ANYTOWN, Any State—XYZ Company today announced the hiring of Sylvia S. Sylvia as office controller. Ms. Sylvia has an associate's degree in business adminstration and will be working out of the home office. XYZ Company was formed by Jim Jackson in 1994 as a home remodeling business, with its goal of creating the kind of living space desirable to people with growing families and to people with families that have already left the nest. Greater use of limited space is one feature of XYZ Company work, while more openess in living styles is another.

With this hiring, XYZ Company positions its owner to spend more time in the field, keeping tabs on quality and rapid growth.

The company is a fully insured, licensed contractor for the state of Any State.

XYZ Company is located at Bumblebee Drive, Anytown, and the phone number is (703) 555–5555.

to be a bit more aggressive here, but you can be almost sure any small-town weekly will be interested in running a profile on you and your new business at some point before, during, or after your start-up. You may find much the same interest at your local daily paper.

THE PUBLIC RELATIONS HOOK

Find what writers and editors call a hook. That's an angle for the story, or as one editor once put it to me, a peg to hang the story on. Do you have an unusual college degree for someone who is a builder? Do you have specific training that makes your company's emphasis special? Is your contracting specialty unusual enough so that it might be the peg for the story? Do you, for example, use special types of wood siding or flooring? Do you install a lot of clerestory windows, greenhouse window inserts, real fireplaces, flagged-floor foyers, atriums, motorized skylights, or redwood or cedar interiors? Be creative, because publicity for you is publicity for your work, and the more publicity you get, the more work you'll get.

WORD OF MOUTH

Marketing is publicity, and publicity comes from many sources, including the most important one: word of mouth. Good word-of-mouth advertising and publicity can carry a company to a crest. On the other hand, unfavorable word-of-mouth publicity can ruin a company. Doing good work is one way to start the tongues wagging in a positive manner, and emphasizing your positive personality traits is another. Working with civic organizations helps, though when you first start your business, you're not really going to have the spare time to do much on the civic front. Join these organizations, of course, but don't commit a lot of your time until your business is reasonably well established.

Try to be pleasant, even when things are going wrong, and turn out the best possible work on all your contracts. You'll note over time that offers are generated by word-of-mouth advertising. Someone asks about a good builder for a particular job, and someone else gives your name. Some builders are at the point, as Steve Arrington is, that people call for a recommendation of *other* builders, because they know Steve is too busy to take on the work they must have done this year, but they respect his judgment. Should you ever get to such a stage, remember that courtesy, in response to what seems a strange request (after all, the other builder is a competitor), is another log added to the wall of your legend, leading to even more word-of-mouth advertising. Eventually you may be able to just about quit advertising, except for that single line in the white pages of your local phone directory. And you may, like Steve Arrington, need a cellular phone to keep from missing out on too much while you run from job site to job site to client to building supply warehouse.

Like every other aspect of the contracting business, success in marketing depends on just how much effort you're willing to put into both the marketing and the overall work that you do.

CHAPTER SIX

YOUR BUSINESS PLAN

Writing a business plan is an excellent way to determine where you stand before you start a business and see where you wish to go. It's easy enough to load the old pickup with tools, run a small ad, and start to land small carpentry jobs without doing much else in the way of planning. But you may find yourself a decade down the road doing the same sorts of small jobs, making the same sort of small-job money, scrambling to get a vehicle that's more reliable and better-quality tools, and wishing you lived in a more comfortable style.

Carpentry work doesn't require the same sort of cheery projections put out by other small businesses, for building and remodeling houses is something that most banks are up on. Your banker probably has a better idea than you of just how much you can make on any one job and how tightly controlled your prices will be by the current construction market. A plan for a home-based carpentry business need not have lengthy financial statements or descriptions of the business. Well-done business plans also help impress bankers while showing them where you stand financially.

A simple business plan allows you to start as small as you like and gives you a clearer idea of what your goals are, so you can work more effectively towards reaching them. It need not be complex, and certainly it is best written in simple language. It effectively provides direction where none may exist, and can simplify your growth as a builder. It can truly simplify the chances you have of getting major loans from banks or other investors who might otherwise figure your chances at succeeding are poor because your planning is not sufficient. If you choose to show your plan to prospective customers, they may find themselves more attracted to specific details, and more likely to contract with you than with a builder who just flies at things haphazardly.

Your business plan needs to cover ways to finance, operate, and profit from your home-based carpentry/building business. It is something that cannot be knocked out on a slow Saturday, but it probably won't take more than a couple of weekends.

You won't need some aspects of the standard business plan. I'm not going to deal with potential mergers and acquisitions, for example, because in all honesty, I haven't got a clue, and don't want one. Most builders I know would shudder at the very idea.

Start by assessing the workability of your prospective business idea. Go over the information in the preceding chapters and check to see if you can meet the requirements of a home-based carpentry business, no matter what its emphasis.

TYPES OF BUSINESS ORGANIZATIONS

You may need to decide on whether or not a proprietorship, partnership, or some form of corporation will work best for your situation. Each has advantages and disadvantages, some of which may be overwhelming.

Single Proprietorship

The most common type of builder's company is the single proprietorship, and that's probably where you will want to start. Its primary advantage is its relative simplicity—all income, above expenses, is classed as your personal income, and is taxed as such. (If you've never worked for yourself before, wait until you get to pay the doubled whack for Social Security, since there is no employer to pick up the second half.) Book-keeping is simple and so is paying taxes. Licensing is also simple; you usually just need a local fictitious-name license. Depending on your desires, you may or may not be bonded, but you must be fully insured when you work as a sole proprietor. The drawback of a sole proprietorship is that in addition to keeping all the money you have left after expenses, you are out in the breeze for any and all possible liabilities. Thus, insurance is imperative, for a single lawsuit can easily bankrupt a small company.

Partnership

A partnership is another way to organize a business. It's not my favorite way of doing things, though for some people, and for me on some jobs, it works well. You don't want to grab a partner because he or she is able to do things you can't: If you can't do all the jobs of a small business, including keeping the books, you shouldn't begin such a business. If a partner offers complementary skills, whether in office or business management or in the field, then the partnership has a chance of succeeding. According to all my sources, you should never take on a partner for a job you can hire someone else to do. In other words, don't go partners with a great bookkeeper. Hire him or her. If you've got a lifelong pal who is a so-so carpenter but has more money to put in the company than you do, walk on by. That kind of situation can only create major problems. Money for start-up can be a problem, but a skilled builder can open up a business with less cash on hand than the owners of many other types of small businesses—assuming that builder gets into an upward-moving construction market.

START-UP COSTS

You need a sufficient amount of cash on hand to provide you with a stable, livable income for at least six months: Starting with less is foolish, for it may take two or three months of trying before you get a job that is large enough to produce decent income. Then you've got to get materials, hire a helper to work with you, and cover other expenses. Better yet, begin with enough to see you through at least one full year.

The size of your working nest egg is determined by the size of your start-up ambitions. If you can live and work for six months on $25,000, all the better, but in many cases more is needed. Helpers have to be paid, tools bought, materials paid for up front if you haven't arranged for credit with local suppliers, and you can bet something is going to go wrong to delay payment on a critically needed completion check before your six months are up. The more cash or credit you have up front, before opening day, the better off you are. You do not need huge amounts of credit, unless you intend building houses on spec for profit.

Finances are something I can't even begin to predict for your home-based carpentry business because I have no idea whether you wish to start tiny and grow to a small or medium size, or start medium and grow huge (or stay the same size). I strongly suggest you start small. Most of us are better adapted to starting small and growing from there. We can select primarily one- and two-person jobs, do them economically and well, and move on to larger jobs as the cash on hand builds up. Generally, clients with smaller jobs are less likely to ask for half a dozen estimates before deciding to start, so you can turn out a round dozen room additions before you even get the contract to build an eight-room house.

Living and construction costs vary so much from area to area, they are impossible to predict. A couple of hundred miles from my home is Washington, D.C. (known here as Gas City), where living costs are almost totally insane. In some respects, though, building costs are lower than they are where I live, which is a rural area. The reason for lower prices for everything from two-by-fours to Sheetrock is simple: competition. You cannot sell a sheet of ⅝-inch CDX for $16 if the outfit down the road is charging $14.50. I have to drive 60 miles one way to save that buck and a half. A builder starting out in Washington, D.C., needs more cash to begin with, however, because housing costs in D.C. are the highest in the nation. Pay is reasonably high in the area, but not astronomical.

You must make accurate estimates and do a lot of checking, particularly early in your business life, to make certain you get the best price for the best quality. If you're setting up your business in an area in which you've lived and worked, you'll already have a major jump on this need, especially if you've worked your way up to lead carpenter for a good company (as I strongly recommend you do before starting your own carpentry business).

Evaluate your business resources. List your assets and skills. What sort of tools do you have? Check your tool needs. Use the tool list I provided earlier as a guide.

PERSONAL FINANCIAL STATEMENT

Name:
Address:
City & State: ZIP:
Telephone:
Date:

ASSETS		LIABILITIES	
Cash		Accounts payable	
Checking accounts		Contracts payable	
		Notes payable	
Savings accounts		Taxes payable	
Stocks			
Bonds		Real estate loans	
Securities			
Real estate		Vehicle loans	
Vehicles		Other liabilities	
Accounts receivable			
Other liquid assets			
TOTAL ASSETS		TOTAL LIABILITIES	
		TOTAL ASSETS	
		TOTAL LIABILITIES	
		NET WORTH (ASSETS MINUS LIABILITIES)	

PERSONAL FINANCIAL STATEMENT

Name: Joe Whizbang
Address: Zip & Zing Street
City & State: Aloysius, KS   ZIP: 33333
Telephone: 805 -555 -1212
Date:

ASSETS		LIABILITIES	
Cash	1,374.00	Accounts payable	3173.91
Checking accounts	22,813. 73	Contracts payable	0.00
		Notes payable	0.00
Savings accounts	38,113.95	Taxes payable	3,913.00
Stocks	0.00		
Bonds	0.00	Real estate loans	137,342.70
Securities	0.00		
Real estate	132,000.00	Vehicle loans	0.00
Vehicles	27,000.00	Other liabilities	0.00
Accounts receivable	0.00		
Other liquid assets	0.00		
TOTAL ASSETS	221,301.68	TOTAL LIABILITIES	144,429.61
		TOTAL ASSETS	221,301.68
		TOTAL LIABILITIES	144,429.61
		NET WORTH (ASSETS MINUS LIABILITIES)	76,872.07

WRITING YOUR BUSINESS PLAN

Make a paper copy of your business plan, for it's hard to hold all the fine points in mind over a period of time. Do the job neatly, on regular typing paper. It needs to be typed if you plan to show anyone else any part of the plan, and, really, it should be typed even if only you are reading it. Make sure your spelling is correct. If you're not using a computer with a word processor and spell checker, use a dictionary. You can find words you can't spell, but the search is harder. Sentences should be short and simple. You're not striving for stylistic greatness here, but for clarity. Many people who may need to look at your business plan are going to come away with an impression of you, so make it neat, tidy, and as accurate as you can, so their main impressions will be of a careful worker with well-thought-out ideas.

Business plans are tools and need to be regarded as such. Too many of us look at them in near terror, because we have the idea that only an MBA from a fancy school can figure one out. If a business plan is laid out so that only an MBA can understand it, it is not doing its work, especially for a builder. It is a challenge to work up a good business plan, but that plan, and its revisions over the years, will help you get a faster start and maintain a faster pace with less confusion. Basically, a business plan sets out your short- and long-term goals for your business and then describes how you're going to get there. In the process, it provides many of the following categories of information, both for your use and for the use of others. If you decide to show clients your business plan, do not show them the financial information.

1. Your business
   a. Description of the business (as full as you can make it)
   b. Marketing methods
   c. Local competition
   d. Operating procedures
2. Financial information
   a. Loan applications
   b. Capital equipment list
   c. Balance sheet
   d. Break-even analysis
   e. Income projections
   f. Cash-flow projections

3. Supporting documents
    a.   Tax returns
    b.   Personal financial statement
    c.   Copies of your license and similar legal documents
    d.   Copy of your résumé
    e.   Copies of letters of acceptance from suppliers who will
            proffer credit

The above outline simply needs expansion along reasonable lines: It is my adaptation of the outline provided by the Small Business Administration, so it certainly covers most of what lending institutions are going to ask you for. Beyond that, the first section can be used alone as a marketing tool, if done well.

Description

When describing your business, cover the types of building you will be doing, and why your skills make you especially suited to those types. Look hard and long at the skills that set you apart from the crowd of builders already out there. The longer you think about this part, the more effective it's going to be. If you have a flair for work that provides extra living comfort at lower cost, say so. If you have a flair for providing the lowest possible cost for luxurious surroundings, say that. Don't be shy. This is where your business marketing program begins.

Marketing and Competition

When describing your marketing plans, explain where you're going to advertise, and why you expect that to be enough. In discussing the local competition, explain how you will do a different job than they can. Do not denigrate your competition. It is not profitable in the long run, for it just builds hard feelings that sometimes never heal.

Your discussion of business operating procedures should include estimates and bids, what kind of crews you work with, and how your labor is hired and paid.

Operating Procedures

The operating procedures section should also cover management. If you're in a working partnership, this is the time to say so, and explain how the partners are going to be doing their different jobs. If you are a corporation, tell who the various officers are, and explain what they'll be doing as the company starts and grows. If, as is most likely, you're going to start as a sole proprietorship, then describe your own business management experience. You have some if you've worked as a lead carpenter, or even if you've only led a framing crew or similar small job segment. Mention how you will apply your experience to providing the best possible work for your clients. This is the place where you really need to brag about all of your abilities, not just those related to management. Your skills are diverse—they have to be to run any small business today. Cover them all, from managing your time effectively to keeping the books to reading the plans for the addition or remodeling job or the homes you're going to build to cutting accurate miters and getting them tightly nailed. Since you're the owner, all the jobs will be yours at the outset. You'll need to emphasize the fact that you are more than capable of doing them all. If you have any doubts, this is not the place to air them. If you have trouble coming up with enough material, discuss your experience. Think over jobs you've worked and go over the things that happened on those jobs, from day-to-day routines to any emergencies you may have helped handle.

Next, discuss your weaknesses. You're bound to have some, and they're probably less important than you think they are, but unless you're the world's greatest builder at your current age, with no room for improvement, there may be some crafts skills you still need to get a handle on. Or you may have problems running a computer. Whatever those weaknesses are, describe them, and then explain how you plan to reduce or eliminate them.

If computer programs drive you nuts, you might consider a course at a local community college. In a short time, I'll be out the door for a 30-mile drive, so I can take my first class in my new word-processing program. Sometime next year, I plan to take a refresher course in cabinetry at a local school. I can build a mighty nice cabinet, but I don't do so with great frequency. For a very few bucks, I get a chance to refresh *all* my woodworking skills, from safety needs to cutting raised panels. It's a bargain, as are most community college and adult education courses. Use them to eliminate your weaknesses.

You will find, and quickly, that having your own business demands that you educate yourself, often on subjects way out of your former range of interests. If you succeed in business, education is going to be a major support on your way to success. The day of the rough-and-ready builder who could drive around in a muddy Caddy, with gloves in one pocket and a tape measure in another, and get by insisting he'd do the "best job you can get, just leave it to me" is long gone. I've seen a number of these "leave it to me" types, and I've never seen one that didn't sooner or later get into major binds because of poor workmanship or an imperfect understanding of the job.

Emphasize your strengths in this section, but describe (briefly) your weaknesses, and discuss how you'll correct these.

Financial Information

Fill out a loan application for and list your capital equipment. A balance sheet may not be necessary, but it is helpful. A break-even analysis is probably a waste of time for a builder. Income and cash-flow projections will be a big help for a new business, if those projections are reasonably accurate. Do not daydream of castles and kings, but make practical, common-sense estimates of the work you expect to obtain, and how you expect to be paid for that work.

Supporting Documents

Your supporting documents will be few when you start up. You won't have a business tax return until you've been in business more than a full fiscal year (simplify your accounting, and make your fiscal year the same as the calendar year), or not before December 31. Your personal financial statement should support your loan applications. Copies of your license and all legal documents should always be readily available to clients, bankers, insurance agents, and others. A copy of your résumé will prove you've got the experience to do the job you want. Finally, if you've managed to persuade local warehouses and various suppliers to extend you

CREDIT APPLICATION

Application No.
Company:
Company Address:
Telephone:
Fax:
Type of Business (Partnership. Corp.):
Years in Business:

PARTNERS OR CORPORATE OFFICERS

Name	Title	Telephone

BANK REFERENCES

Bank Name & Address	Contact Name & Phone	Account Number(s)

TRADE REFERENCES

I certify that the above information is true. This information is to be used only for opening an account.

Signature	Title	Date

thirty-day net credit, see if they will write short notes to that effect. It will simplify your applications for other credit if you are already considered creditworthy by some of those who will be providing you with materials on a near-daily basis.

OTHER USES FOR A BUSINESS PLAN

Business plans require more material to be useful over a long period of time and for jobs other than getting an immediate line of credit.

A business plan lets you set up a timetable for yourself, evaluate your physical and fiscal resources, and helps to set your prices. It also makes it easier to set realistic goals, knocking the air castles down where they belong and helping you make practical plans for the future. In fact, a properly done business plan forces you to examine yourself, your resources, and your general plans objectively enough to accurately assess the feasibility of your plan to go into business for yourself. In some cases, a business plan may convince you to back off for the time being. On the other hand, it may convince you to start larger than you'd first planned. Setting tough goals makes sense. Setting unattainable goals results in long-term problems. Goals that are easily attained also create problems by slowing potential business growth. You'll learn to judge the edges more accurately as time goes on, and your projections will grow more accurate. If you're tough-minded and careful, your projections will be workable and useful.

BUSINESS PLANNING HELP

There are books that will help you with business plan forms, most of which are easily and quickly adaptable to small builders' businesses. There are also a few business plan programs for home computers. I haven't examined any of these in depth and hesitate to recommend one over another.

The six planners I describe below can help you summarize your business goals and project profits, but you will still have to do a lot of work. Again, you are not going to be preparing a plan that takes a totally unknown business from conception to final incorporation and acceptance on the New York Stock Exchange. For that sort of business, the lender is the final audience for the business plan and the plan must be complete down to the last nickel of projected revenue, cost, and profit. You won't need to be so precise.

These half-dozen plans offer slightly different variations on the standard business plan. My evaluations are based on reading descriptive material rather than personal experience. You may want to supplement them with your own research. In fact, I suggest you do.

BizPlan Builder is from Jian Tools for Sales, and has been around since 1988. The disk builds Word or WordPerfect files, and data is presented in Lotus 1-2-3 spreadsheet format. The plan is difficult to use and seems aimed at getting too much information down on paper. You can of course, delete anything that doesn't apply to your new business. It's priced at $129. Phone (800) 346–5426.

Business Blueprint is from an outfit called Spreadware, and works with the Excel 4.0 and later databases. The package is costly at $149 for a single disk. There are a dozen finance-related charts, far more, really, than a start-up builder is going to need. The manual lacks information on the business planning process, the templates are all for Macintosh format, and you will almost certainly find yourself gathering more data than you need. Phone (619) 347–2365.

Business Plan Toolkit covers everything from financial analysis to market forecasting. There are forty-six topics to cover in the text writer area, and a large set of spreadsheet templates. The manual is said to be super complete, with a great deal of good advice on preparing a business plan. This one may be a lot more than start-up builders need, especially at $149.95, but it does a good and complete job. Phone (800) 229–7526.

First Step Business Plan is a product of the National Business Association, in Dallas. This one can't give you a balance sheet (which you almost certainly don't need anyway), but it does provide modules (free to members) for a profit or loss statement, cash-flow analysis, and a review. This association, and its $5.00-per-disk programs, may be worthwhile for some start-up builders. Phone (800) 456–0440.

PlanMaker is from PowerSolutions for Business. The interface is menu-driven and easy to use, with three sample business plans provided as guides. It doesn't include a spreadsheet component, but it has financial tables to help you organize projected operating expenses, amortization of loans, and an overall balance sheet. You pull the figures in from elsewhere, which is okay for builders. The split-screen text editor has the instructions in the top half, and the information is entered, by you, in the bottom half. The price is $129. Phone (800) 955–3337.

Plan Write for Business from Business Resource Software includes a full-featured word processor with a spell checker, a business plan outliner (where has this feature been!), and a spreadsheet module. You even get a business-term glossary, and much advice for various elements of your plan. The final report is good-looking and does a better job of meeting generally approved standards than do the preceding programs. Plan Write costs $129.95. Phone (800) 423–1228.

A note on computer programs: Call the above numbers to get further information about these products. Do not ever order a computer program, unless it's an early release of an upgrade, directly from the company that produces it. Order from a local computer retailer or discount office-supply house and you will save up to 45 percent off the retail price, an appreciable difference.

COMPLETING YOUR BUSINESS PLAN

Before any business plan is useful, it must be put in finished form. There are probably as many finished forms as there are business plans, but if you're not using a computerized setup, you'll need to type or word process your final form. I suggest you beg or borrow a word processor and computer. Pay a few bucks to have it done, if you aren't going to computerize. The range of visual expression in the form of fonts is much greater, and a good laser printer turns out pages that look typeset, which is much to be desired when you're trying to impress the socks off somebody.

In addition, make sure the finished form is in polished language. By polished I don't mean bright, shiny, show-off language, but good, workmanlike English, with no misspellings, clumsy sentences, and grammatical errors. If you've got a problem writing that sort of English, hire someone to help. There are many high school teachers out there who welcome the chance to make a few extra dollars doing something they're supposed to be good at. (Not all are, so check carefully.)

Confidential Business Plan

Plane & Saw Builders
1415 Beaufort Lane
Sacre Bleu, WI 77793

Telephone: (123) 555-7733
Fax: (123) 555-7737

Owner: Slim Whittler

Confidential Business Plan

Copy Number_____

Remember that long and fancy words don't make a favorable impression—they irritate you when other people use them, right? Well, then, don't do the same to others. Avoid as much jargon as possible, and leave the buzzwords for others—*Power, empowerment,* and *the "I"* (or any other letter) word are among the worst at the moment.

Even if you are good at writing, get a proofreader. I'm always amazed at the number of typographical and other errors I find in my own writing when I go back to it in a week or two.

A cover page is essential. Because this is a limited-edition business plan, I suggest enclosing the entire plan in a clear plastic cover, as well. It will keep the business plan from showing premature wear and tear.

I'm not sure the copy number helps anything but your ability to keep track of the limited number of copies you should turn out. Make a note in a ledger of some sort just where each copy went, and when that person got the copy.

Table of Contents

A table of contents is simply a restatement of your outline, listing the various parts of the business plan. With a word processor, you can easily list page numbers for each section.

Executive Summary

The executive summary is just what it says, a quick summary of the entire document, with the kernel of each section presented in short and simple words. It is most effective if you can keep the entire summary to no more than one page. The executive summary serves as a pointer, telling the person who reads the summary whether or not he or she wants to go on and read in more detail what you are going to do and how you plan to do it. It saves time for the person reviewing your business plan. (This is the only part of the business plan I didn't include in the SBA-derived outline.)

Business Description

Provide details of the business, from the specifics of ownership—proprietorship, partnership, or corporation—to the number of employees (if any). Explain the reason the business exists and how it functions. Next discuss your strengths, as you see them. If you have a business philosophy, discuss it. Back off technical details of building, but describe clearly the types of building you do or expect to do shortly. Describe where you stand now and where you intend to be in one year's time, two years' time, and five years' time. Do not use the word hope to describe your intentions. Write about the present range of your business and its direction. You can discuss your operating hours, but those are seldom important with your kind of work, as you know. You work until the work is done or the light is gone some days, and other days the weather drives you off the job.

Your Financial Plan

This is the point where you get your loan applications together, list capital equipment, make up your balance sheet, and do the income and cash-flow projections. If you're aiming to use loans at any point during the first couple of years of your business, this is the most important part of your business plan. Even if you don't expect to be using loans, you surely will be needing credit from suppliers.

The balance sheet is essentially the statement of your financial condition, and I've enclosed a sample here to help you put together an accurate one. Adapt it to suit your needs, lengthening it, or abbreviating it.

Begin your financial plan with a short narrative of your financial condition. Since you are a beginning builder, this is the only part of your financial statement that can be accurate. Everything else is a projection, an educated guess. You may need to state sources of funds here, if you've gotten funds from anywhere other than your own savings. The break-even analysis is nothing more than an estimate of when that will happen, and is based on two projections described below, profit or loss and cash flow.

Funds Sources

You may wish to add a listing of the sources of your funds as further information for bankers and others who may well want to know what they're going to be loaning money against. This is a tool that can be overused, but a reasonable listing of where you got the funds to purchase each item or group of items (such as hammers and saws) and how much and where you got capitalization for other things is sometimes as helpful as the overall balance sheet, which doesn't include such details.

You can easily see that anyone noting your savings and investments and the amount you've already invested in getting ready to start your business would be impressed with your seriousness. Coming as close as possible to the higher ends of your estimates doesn't hurt at all when you go looking for more money for the business. Obtaining 20 or 30 thousand dollars to have on hand as a contingency fund against unforeseen costs is a good idea and might be a reason to approach an investor with your business plan.

Profit and Loss (Income) Projections

For the business plan, you will need profit or loss projections for a full year, done on a monthly basis. You'll also need quarterly projections for the second year and annual projections for the third, fourth, and fifth years. If you start in midyear, project the months remaining in that year

_____

ASSETS
LIABILITIES

    Cash:

        Bank Accounts $ _____

        Accounts Payable $ _____

    Accounts Receivable Short-term notes $ _____

    Taxes payable $ _____

    Payroll $ _____

    Total Current Assets $ _____

    Long-term investments $ _____

    Land Buildings (cost)

    Owner's equity (assets minus liabilities) $ _____

    Less depreciation $ _____

    Net value $ _____

TOTAL LIABILITIES $ _____

FIXED ASSETS

    Furniture/fixtures $ _____

    Less depreciation $ _____

    Net value $ _____

    Vehicles $ _____

    Less Allowance for Depreciation $ _____

TOTAL FIXED ASSETS $ _____

TOTAL ASSETS $ _____

NET WORTH (Owner's Equity) $ _____

LIABILITIE⌐ & NET WORTH $ _____

SOURCES OF FUNDS		
Assets	Amount (Cost)	Source
Cash		
Investments		
Accounts receivable		
Materials & supplies		
Vehicle		
Furniture & fixtures		
Office equipment		
Tools		

and all of the following year on a monthly basis. A properly done profit and loss (P and L) projection can be the basis for a lot of other solid information and give you a very good idea of just how your business is going to do.

At the outset all P and L statements are projections, but as you progress in your business, profit and loss quarterly reports are superb devices for tracking expenses and income, allowing you to quickly figure out where you stand. Most computerized bookkeeping programs provide such reports quickly, accurately, and far more easily than if you have to make them up yourself.

Cash-Flow Projections

Cash-flow projections can tell you if and when you can afford some new tool or a trip to the Outer Banks or Hawaii. They are similar to P and L statements, but differ in several ways, including the way finances are handled: Your cash-flow projections, and later your reports, concern only the cash on hand. If it hasn't arrived yet, then it doesn't exist as far as the cash-flow reports are concerned. Of course, with projections, you must "guesstimate" about how much you're going to receive at any one time. For decades, I've misjudged on this one vital aspect of a business: Too often I believe those fateful words, "the check's in the mail" or "is being cut," so my cash-flow projections are always far too optimistic. Don't let that happen to you; it makes for great problems in dealing with your expenses. If anything, learn my lesson early, and learn it well: Take a pes-

PROFIT & LOSS STATEMENT

	Jan.	Feb.	Mar.	First Quarter Totals
Construction revenue				
Cabinetry revenue				
Total revenue:				
Cost of goods sold:				
Materials and supplies				
Outside labor				
Miscellaneous				
Total cost of goods sold:				
GROSS PROFIT:				
EXPENSES:				
Wages/salaries				
Payroll deductions				
Advertising				
Vehicle				
Depreciation				
Insurance				
Interest paid				
Legal and professional fees				
Office expenses				
Rent or lease				
Repairs & maintenance				
Supplies				
Permits & licenses				
Tools				
Travel & entertainment				
Utilities				
Telephone				
Postage				
Dues & publications				
Printing & copying				
Trash pickup				
Miscellaneous				
TOTAL EXPENSES:				
NET PROFIT (LOSS)				

simistic approach to projecting cash flow. Sooner or later, you'll find your lack of faith is justified, because the client you like most is going to be the one with a check that resembles a Ping-Pong ball or is perpetually delayed. This will be the person who tells you he or she didn't cause your financial problems. Which is true enough, because if you had any sense, you would fold your tent on his (or her) work until the money is in hand. If you have repeat jobs brought in by a late payer, I'd suggest getting all money up front, but under no circumstances get less than 50 percent.

CHECK ACTIVITY BEFORE STARTING

Check your locality for activity in the construction trades. If a lot of houses are going up, it's easier to get into residential construction. If times are bad, check out remodeling, repairing, upgrading (insulation and various venting options come to mind, but there are many other choices), and additions. Remodeling and putting up additions are also excellent ways to go into "up" housing markets. Remodeling jobs are more extensive in good times, and additions are usually larger. There will also be more jobs available, thus increasing your activity. As activity increases, profits increase.

Decide what you want, and go for it, starting as small as necessary, but as large as practical. You may find yourself in one of those infrequent periods when small builders have a lot more trouble getting work than larger builders. Usually a good, small job contractor or builder will do well no matter what the economy is like, but on occasion, the person specializing in small remodeling jobs gets very little work because most of the available jobs in the area are new construction and large remodeling jobs. If things are really bad, even large, established builders may start looking and bidding for the small jobs to keep their experienced crews working together so that they're still on hand when the next upswing arrives.

Examine your location carefully for the most advantageous start-up size, and then begin your financial planning, making decisions on where to get the money you know you'll need to live on and pay business bills with for at least six months (a year is better).

CASH FLOW REPORT

	Jan.	Feb.	Mar.	First Quarter Totals
CASH ON HAND (1st of Month)				
CASH RECEIPTS				
a: Collected receivables				
b: Other				
TOTAL CASH RECEIPTS				
CASH EXPENDITURES				
Gross wages				
Taxes				
Materials				
Supplies (office, etc.)				
Subcontracts				
Repairs & maintenance				
Advertising				
Vehicle				
Travel & entertainment				
Accounting				
Legal				
Rent				
Telephone				
Utilities				
Printing & copying				
Postage				
Shipping (UPS, FedEx, etc.)				
Insurance				
Dues & publications				
Miscellaneous				
Other				
Subtotal				
Capital expenditures				
TOTAL CASH PAID				
CASH POSITION				

FINANCING YOUR START-UP

The decisions on how to finance a company start-up, no matter how small, need a lot of thought. Running it out of your own savings until you can start paying yourself a salary is obviously the best way. Running a company start-up from savings means you risk only your own money, not family money, and not money belonging to other people, as is the case when you borrow money to meet short-term goals.

Part of your calculation should be the desirable size of a start-up carpentry business in your area. If you feel the time is perfect for a start-up as a small builder, and can prove that to yourself and others with real figures, then you can consider forming your own company even though you're short of cash. Staying short of cash is always a good way to get in a great deal of trouble, but there are avenues open to most responsible people who want to start out bigger than a one-truck, one-saw, one-project builder. If your business plans presents all the facts straightforwardly and in a neat and concise manner, then you've got a great shot at getting going with borrowed money.

STATEMENT OF REVENUES & EXPENSES

For the Month Ending:_____

REVENUES
Sales Receipts	$_____	
Commissions/fees/royalties	$_____	
Contributions	$_____	
Investment income	$_____	
Other revenues	$_____	
TOTAL REVENUES		$_____

EXPENSES
Employee salaries	$_____	
Commissions	$_____	
Rent	$_____	
Utilities	$_____	
Materials	$_____	
Office supplies	$_____	
Advertising	$_____	
Travel and entertainment	$_____	
Professional services	$_____	
Dues and subscriptions	$_____	
Meetings and conferences	$_____	
Communications	$_____	
Insurance	$_____	
Banking fees	$_____	
Depreciation	$_____	
Donations	$_____	
Taxes	$_____	
Other expenses	$_____	
TOTAL EXPENSES		$_____

EXCESS OF REVENUES OVER EXPENSES $_____

STATEMENT OF REVENUES & EXPENSES

For the Month Ending: 12/31/97

REVENUES

Sales Receipts	$ 8,000	
Commissions/fees/royalties	$ 18,000	
Contributions	$ 4,500	
Investment income	$ 7,500	
Other revenues	$ 6,600	
TOTAL REVENUES		$44,600

EXPENSES

Employee salaries	$ 7,000	
Commissions	$ 1,500	
Rent	$ 10,800	
Utilities	$ 1,800	
Materials	$ 265	
Office supplies	$ 125	
Advertising	$ 4,250	
Travel and entertainment	$ 800	
Professional services	$ 350	
Dues and subscriptions	$ 125	
Meetings and conferences	$ 575	
Communications	$ 60	
Insurance	$ 775	
Banking fees	$ 180	
Depreciation	$ 4,500	
Donations	$ 3,800	
Taxes	$ 150	
Other expenses	$ 1,400	
TOTAL EXPENSES		$ 38,455

EXCESS OF REVENUES OVER EXPENSES $ 6,145

CHAPTER SEVEN

FINDING GOOD HELP

G etting and keeping good help can be something of a problem when the time comes for you to grow a bit. You need, though, to know how to attract honest, trained, or trainable employees, and how to keep them. Getting an employee is easy: Getting an employee you wish to continue working with is harder. It is made difficult by the customary practice of hiring independent contractors on a day or job rate, when what you really need is a reliable person who shows up daily, at the time specified, and does the work cheerfully and well.

CASUAL LABOR

Casual labor is often a great help to the new business, and I don't mean to knock it for those just beginning who only occasionally need another person to hold up the end of a board or help with some of the rougher work, such as carrying materials from delivery or cutting site to actual work site. But today casual labor is generally more troublesome for the careful builder than it is helpful. I've done casual labor; my first carpentry jobs were on that basis. Back in those years, though, employing casual labor was a whole lot simpler than it is now. My boss hired me for the day, paid me at day's end, and if I owed taxes on the $10 or so, it was my worry.

Today you cannot expect to get away with under-the-table payments, at least with any frequency, when hiring casual labor. Sooner or later the IRS is apt to learn of what you're doing from either the laborer or someone else. When that happens, you are on an endless belt of troubles. Cover yourself today by keeping your hiring practices legal. It's worth the effort of filing a few forms and paying your half of the employee's Social Security (FICA), which is currently 7.65 percent.

You must, then, first settle on the type of help you need: casual or permanent. If you need only occasional labor for your first months in business, then work out a method of hiring the best local casual laborers—there's always a pool of this sort of talent, willing and ready to work a week or ten days at a clip in hopes of a full-time, permanent job at the end of that time. Some are well worth hiring permanently, some aren't.

TEMPORARY EMPLOYMENT CONTRACTORS

In addition to casual and permanent labor, there is a third option today, one getting more and more popular—temporary employment contractors. I honestly don't know how many craftspeople work through temporary outfits. These places once were for office temps only, and were superb for replacements for vacationing secretaries and bookkeepers. Today Manpower, among many others, frequently advertises for factory help. The advantage to you here is that the temp employer is the employer on record, and you are simply a contractor with that employer. Thus, they take over the advertising, interviewing, and general processing as well as all the bookkeeping for temporary help.

The disadvantage is that temporary employee firms have to charge more than you might otherwise pay. They've got a considerable overhead, for many offer full benefits to their employees after a specific period of working time in addition to providing you with all record-keeping services. Their hourly rate may be as much as 175 percent of what you'd pay the same employee if you hired him or her directly. These employment contractors do, however, save you from the complexities of hiring and record keeping. They reduce all the hassle I am about to describe to a single weekly check, paid to the employment contractor. If such contractors are available and you need help for a few weeks on a larger than usual job, you'll be in good shape. You can, if you like the person's work, always hire the temp away from the employment contractor. That's an expected part of the business, and a fringe benefit for some of the temps who want full-time work.

It all works out, even if your $10-an-hour temp costs you $15 per hour with the help of a contractor. Hiring on your own, you'd end up paying another 76 cents for Social Security and would also have to handle withholding tax paperwork and pay unemployment and disability insurances, too. All in all, the $15 per hour you pay the temp contractor might cost you $1.00, maybe $1.25, and you save all the bookkeeping and record-keeping work. And if the IRS ever comes back at you, you just point them at the temp contractor!

INDEPENDENT CONTRACTORS

In some ways, independent contractors, or subcontractors, are the easiest to work with of all. Like you they're self-employed and get paid by the job, which they do under contract. Sooner or later, you are going to work with subcontractors, either as a sub yourself or as a contractor hiring several subs to complete a job. Very few builders today go into a job planning to do everything from the site layout to driving the last roofing nail themselves. In fact the average residential job requires a site prep crew, a foundation crew, a framing crew, a wiring crew, a plumbing crew, an insulation crew, a drywall crew, a cabinet-hanging crew, painters, siding mechanics, and a roofing crew. Most contractors install their own windows and doors, but a few might not. On some residential jobs there are bricklayers and stonemasons and specialty stair-building crews. A rural site may have a well-drilling crew and a septic-field crew.

Many builders confine their actual work to site layout, framing, and finish carpentry. All else is subbed out. There are many variations on this theme, though. What you do and what you sub out are decisions you need to make as you go along. At the start, you may sub out almost all of your larger jobs to avoid investing in expensive tools (price a backhoe and a Ditch Witch to see what doing your own site work costs) and carrying a large, expensive labor force on your books.

Subcontractors are available for every specialty you can imagine, and they're the lifeblood of the small-building industry in the United States. Proper use of subs can help you get off to a flying start as a home-based carpenter or builder.

Selecting Subcontractors

If you've been working for any reasonable length of time in your area, you have a good idea of the strengths and weaknesses of many of the local subcontractors. I strongly suggest you make a written list of these subs and their particular strengths. Do not write down anything truly derogatory in a file that may be seen by someone else. Emphasize strengths in a manner that will indicate to you what the weaknesses, if any, of a particular sub might be.

The low-ball subcontractor on any job may be the best one for the job, but you should take a good look at that sub's record. Low bids aren't always the best bids. Get recommendations for subcontractors who are new to you by checking with friends in the trades and, if you're on good terms, with local building inspectors. Building inspectors get to see the work of most of the subcontractors in a city, town, or county on an almost daily basis. They also know what makes up a good job, so they quickly come to know which subcontractors do the best work and are most often on time. (Building inspectors have to set up an inspection schedule, so they know who's behind and who isn't.) Other builders may also give you tips if you call and ask.

Check references for any subcontractor, comparing the subcontractor's claims against actual job performance as rated by the contractor. Check the credit the subcontractor has with suppliers. If his or her suppliers shut credit down in the middle of your job, you're going to have to pony up or accept work delays while the sub straightens things out.

Keeping Your Subs

Keeping good subcontractors is as important as keeping good crews, for a good subcontractor who consistently turns in good work on time and on budget can make you look better and add quality to the project. If you get good people working for you, try to award them jobs whenever possible instead of choosing low bidders each time. You may feel you're saving with the low bidders, but paying a few dollars more for the certainty of top-quality work is often worth far more than the extra money.

A poor subcontractor, or a good one working below par, can ruin the schedule of an entire job and sometimes more than that. If your electricians are overbooked and don't show up to run the wiring, your insulation sub can't get in and place the batts, which sets the drywall sub back, which . . . well, you see, and I'm sure you already know. The subs who should come later are thrown off their schedules, which can force them to drop your job or schedule it much later. In the process, your job ends up costing you more money, thus reducing profits.

All-Purpose Crews

This scheduling problem occurs with too much frequency, and it is the reason many small builders try to hire crews that have all the skills to do each and every job. I don't drive heavy equipment—backhoes and such—and refuse to even drive a farm tractor. I swear I'm the only nail driver I've ever known who doesn't drive at least a Ditch Witch. There are days I wish I did.

But in general, I don't feel hiring all-purpose crews is as cost-effective as working with a crew that does the carpentry well and leaves the specialties to the specialists. Just try to make sure that you don't pay either time or cash premiums because of someone else's scheduling foul-ups.

Spreading the Risk

There's another advantage to hiring subcontractors: You are spreading the risk. You're going to find estimating carpentry materials and labor enough of a challenge (in other words, an opportunity to screw up). Do you really know enough, or want to know enough, to spec and estimate the costs of concrete, wiring, and plumbing needs? Concrete is the simplest to spec of the three, since its estimates are based on simple cubic volume, but getting it right can be tough—and so can getting the surfaces of concrete floors right if you don't have the tools and experience to do the job properly. It isn't something you can come back and sand down for another try.

In addition to doing the job better, subcontractors can often do the job for less money than you can. They buy from their suppliers in greater bulk than you can, so their materials cost less. Their higher labor costs are offset by the much greater speed of that labor: Just for kicks, try laying brick alongside an accomplished bricklayer, someone like my nephew

Nicky Nowland, who subcontracts out of the Brooklin, Maine, area. If you can keep up for the first fifteen minutes, you're better than 95 percent of the general builders out there. Thirty minutes later, you'll be in the same hole as the rest of them, and your work will get messier and messier as you go, while Nicky's starts out neat, stays neat, and finishes neat. In one-third the time.

FULL-TIME EMPLOYEES

Finding good crew members is difficult much of the time, but once you have, if you treat your workers well, the turnover will be low. Be choosy in selecting your employees, as they should be in selecting their employer, and you'll both be satisfied. Pay and benefits are important considerations, but you also need to check out attitude and expertise to match the range of your projects.

Crew Size

Crew size is up to you. Most of us start with one helper and move on to larger crews as time and finances permit. Around here, Steve Arrington (an accomplished builder) works mostly with three-man crews, sometimes goes to four, and seldom drops to two. He shifts between two or more jobs most of the time and needs the extra help. Other local builders use two-man crews, with the lead being a worker. Remodelers often work with just one helper for their entire careers.

Legal Considerations

I'm not going to cover every aspect of legal and sensible employment, in part because I can't. Individual states have varying requirements, and you must adhere to those of your locality. The federal government has a few requirements, especially in the area of taxation, and you'd best pay attention. Job-site safety is another federal concern, though the government is less worried about small builders than other businesses. That doesn't mean you should ignore the needs of safety, because a safe site is a more profitable site, if no other reason appeals. Lost time due to injury means lost time on the job, period. And lost time costs money. You will also find it easier to keep employees, impress prospective clients, keep your insurance costs down, and generally get along better.

Finding Job Candidates

Finding a group of candidates for the job or jobs you have open is just a start, but it's a start you must make. Probably the best place to post ads for carpenters is at your suppliers. Sooner or later, a carpenter has to come to the supplier. You can also get references from friends and neighbors (which sometimes work out, but usually don't) and you can advertise in the local newspapers. Newspaper ads are a last resort, for they tend to bring in large numbers of applicants, some totally inexperienced.

You can tap any market, anywhere, for full-time work: Let's not forget that Harrison Ford was a successful carpenter for years before he went on to being a supremely successful whip wielder in movies. Check Actors' Equity, and similar groups, where you may find that people waiting to make it in one career are well versed in paying their bills with other skills, including carpentry.

If you're unable to find the people you want from recommendations or sheets pinned up on the building supply bulletin boards, and you decide to advertise in a newspaper, you'll need a quick and reasonably reliable way to sort through the responses.

You may also have found good workers from the temporary employment services mentioned earlier. If so, check and see if your temp or temps will consider full-time, all-the-time permanence. You already know what they're worth on your jobs.

Whether you're in the market for a lead carpenter or a crew member, you have to do a fast sorting job. Asking the crew applicants to do a few simple chores around the job site may give you a quick reading. If someone is unable to lift a sheet of plywood or length of two-by-four material, then obviously, you can't work with him or her. If those initial jobs are done quickly and easily, move on to asking your applicants to pick up lengths of one material or another and bring them back to you. If they can't find things or bring the wrong sizes, they're unsuitable for your crew. It's essential to know whether an applicant can drive half a dozen nails straight and use a square, handsaw, and circular saw.

Do a quick run-through of the basics any carpenter needs to know, but do those only after checking to see if the person is bright enough to follow simple instructions and strong enough to do the work. Skills can be learned and pay may be adjusted accordingly if they are lacking, but if basic intelligence—or interest—isn't there, you can do nothing with that person.

Naturally, you should check all references supplied. In today's world, you almost never get a "Joe Soso is a rotten carpenter" type of reference. We're too litigious, and even if the statement is true, the person giving that reference is apt to be sued by Joe Soso should Joe ever find out what was said.

When a reference isn't out-and-out favorable and enthusiastic, you have to listen to intonation and pay attention to the topics that aren't mentioned. Evasions to questions about whether or not the referenced company would consider rehiring the candidate are telltale, too. Even if the job candidate did nothing outstanding, nothing to make previous employers jump up and down with enthusiasm and weep when he left, Joe Soso may still be a perfectly suitable carpenter, and you may be able to motivate him. If he also has a record of staying on jobs for short periods and moving on, ask him why, and ask yourself if you believe his answer. Some sort of stable approach to work life is essential for anyone who is past their early twenties. Similar approaches need to be used to garner information, and much is done in a conversational manner.

Start with an employment application similar to the one included here, but go on to emphasize considerations that are important to you and your work, and see how the applicant responds.

The sample application is a guide, and you can request additional information that you feel you need for a specific job: Do not, under any circumstance, in person, on the phone, or in writing, ask questions pertaining to race, religion, age, or sex. Period. I'm told that questions about weight are also taboo, as are those about physical condition, though how you can hire a carpenter with a huge weight problem or another physical disability, I don't know. Check with your lawyer before setting up your final employment questionnaire. What you can legally ask about and what you think about may be two decidedly different matters. There is no sense at all hiring someone who can't do the job.

Finding Lead Carpenters

If you're looking for a lead carpenter, you've got to do more work. Your ad will bring the good, the bad, and some who are indifferent, and you want the best of the good.

To hire your lead carpenter, you need to know much more about an applicant's intent, skills, and background. Motivation is an important attribute in a lead carpenter, for without very good motivation, your lead is not going to do the job. If you're lucky, your carpenters and your lead will work well together without a lot of back-and-forth about things, but sooner or later, the lead needs to prove his or her skills, because sooner or later, on every job, there is something the journeyman isn't quite sure of, and questions are asked. If the lead knows, or can figure it out, all is well. If not, you have problems with a lead who can't lead. In-depth knowledge of the craft of carpentry is an absolute essential for your lead.

Extreme forcefulness isn't necessary or, considering how tetchy many carpenters are about being pushed instead of led, desirable much of the time. An equable, firm personality is about right, as are good personal habits (neat hair, clean work clothes, vehicle, and person). Skills and attitudes can be checked in the course of conversation. Has this person been a lead before? Can the person lead both beginners and journey-level workers?

Check some skills: Ask the applicant to lay out stair stringers or, if your current job calls for it, valley jack rafters for a hip roof. Check on the applicant's methods of planning a day on the job. If you're working on finish carpentry, have the prospective lead lay out and cut some crown molding. Whatever job is available, ask the applicant to take a shot at the most difficult phase of that job.

Assuming an applicant for carpenter or lead carpenter makes a fine impression and you feel pretty good about his or her abilities, talk over your company policies, and see what the applicant thinks of how you now treat or intend to treat employees. If the picture seems to please, give him or her a ninety-day tryout, with the understanding that the job is to be permanent if all goes well, but with no warning or reasons needed, on either side, if things don't work out.

You'll find some people don't meet expectations from day one. Others do and fade in the stretch, running well behind the field by the

EMPLOYMENT APPLICATION
STAIR & CASE, BUILDERS

PERSONAL INFORMATION

Name: _____ Date: _____

Social Security Number: _____

Home address: _____

City, State, Zip: _____

Home phone: _____ Business phone: _____

US citizen? _____ If not, give visa no. _____

_____ and expiration: _____

POSITION APPLIED FOR

Title: _____ Salary desired: _____

Referred by: _____ Date available: _____

EDUCATION

High School (name, city, state): _____

Graduation date: _____

College, business, or technical schools: _____

Dates attended: _____

PREVIOUS EMPLOYERS

Date: _____

Date: _____

Date: _____

REFERENCES

_____

_____

_____

third or fourth week. If the applicant is doing well at the end of three months, you've got a find and should make him or her permanent as quickly as possible.

Holidays

About seventy-five years ago, a fair day's work brought a fair day's pay, and that was it. Though the wide array of benefits introduced after World War II is decreasing in size these days because of cost, you still have a strong responsibility to your employees and to yourself to offer more than just a job. Coverage for disabilities and job injuries and payment of Social Security taxes are, as mentioned earlier, legally mandated. You'll have to offer more to attract the exceptionally skilled and talented people you want to employ.

You know you're going to let employees take some holidays off, so make them a formal part of working conditions, instead of letting the employee guess, as a lot of small builders do.

"Hey, we going to get the Friday after Thanksgiving off?"

"If it rains."

That's nonsense, and not good employee policy. It's also known as jerking your employees around, and good carpenters are going to stand for only so much of that before they're down the road on another job. List at least five holidays, and preferably more. The old familiars come to mind: July 4, Labor Day, Thanksgiving, Christmas, and New Year's Day. Use these and two or three more of your choosing. Make your selections and stick to them, knowing that days off will cost you some money but that your crew will be happier for getting more than the bare minimum of legal holidays.

Sick days are variable. Some companies offer three or four; government agencies tend to offer the most and let them accumulate. You might try allowing three or four sick days, with pay, and three personal days, which are fairly standard among larger businesses.

All of this costs money, but it also helps you keep your employees once you've gone through the hassle of finding them, interviewing them, hiring them, and getting them to work in a manner you like (or getting yourself used to the way they work).

Health Insurance

The most expensive benefit is health insurance, and it is one I recommend you supply. There are now some tax breaks available, even for small businesses, and soon there may be a real change in the escalation of health-care costs. I doubt, though, we're going to see major cost reductions in insurance until some basic issues are resolved. For example, recently a spate of people have insisted the insurance companies pay for experimental treatments for cancer, though the treatments have almost no chance of success. Companies have refused, but courts are increasingly forcing payment.

That being said, you need to supply some form of health benefits to your employees. Some won't need them, but to make them available to yourself, you must make them available to employees. You can do two things: Shop around for the best program for the money, which means you, as a small businessperson, almost certainly must avoid Blue Cross and Blue Shield. Let your employees carry part of the cost of your program. If you get a good, reasonably priced program and pick up, for example, 60 percent of the cost, your carpenters save considerably over enrolling individually.

Pay

Hourly rates vary from one region to another and even from job to job, so I won't suggest any dollar amounts. There is a point to be made for paying slightly over the going rate for a given job, but the point must be made gently.

To keep and get good people, you must offer competitive wages, and that's only fair. It impresses employees if you offer the straight, competitive hourly rates they expect, and then offer a 10 to 20 percent raise at the end of ninety days. I'd suggest starting at 10 percent at the end of the trial period, allowing yourself higher percentages for truly exceptional people who in a short time work themselves into your routines so well you cannot bear the thought of losing them.

Make sure you've got a standard pay policy for raises and rewards. My wife left a job she liked for a very simple reason: no raise, and no talk of one, though she got many compliments on her work from the boss, and increasing responsibility. Some trade publications suggest that trips to shows and similar rewards can replace raises. Forget it. It simply isn't true.

Incentive Plans

Incentive plans work well with most employees. Give some thought to sharing a percentage of the profits with those who help you earn them. Incentive plans are also helpful in keeping people working year-round.

Most incentive plans work on a per job basis, with a profit pool distributed to employees if all stipulations are met. Those stipulations must include the job running on schedule, under budget, and free of collection problems. Savings can be distributed to employees, including the office staff, if any. A monthly payout is probably best, as it makes minimum accounting demands, yet provides a fair frequency of reward, so your employees know when they'll be getting the extra money they've earned.

Incentives in the form of bonuses can help retain workers throughout the year. Start the worker below the prevailing wage, with a promise of 52 weeks work at that wage. Then tell the worker that there will be bonuses that bring his (or her) wage up to or even above the current prevailing wage. The basis incentive is 52 weeks of pay at a wage that may be as much as 33 percent below the prevailing wage. The percentage may vary depending on your locale. Hawaii, Florida, and California and some other areas don't fit the idea too well, and those places with short winters don't work, either. Builders who keep busy every winter regardless of weather also won't need this plan.

Money is the main motivator for much work, and it's unfortunate that too many owners of small businesses who are themselves primarily motivated by money (would you clean septic tanks for nothing?) don't realize that others, regardless of skills, abilities, and love for the job, also receive a good boost of adrenaline when cashing a weighty paycheck.

Money is also a way of keeping score. The person whose hourly pay is raised a buck an hour when everyone else gets half that knows he or she is leading the game.

In essence, if you pay each and every person what he or she is worth, you're going to have a mass of angry people. Well, that's the old joke, anyway. In the building business, you can make enough money to treat your employees well and still do well yourself, on a modest scale. (You're not Donald Trump and aren't likely to be in the same league while running a home-based carpentry business.) As employees become more efficient, doing what they do with greater speed and fewer mistakes, it pays for you to reward them. If you don't, someone else probably will, sooner or later.

Employee Policies

Treat your employees as you'd like an employer to treat you, and you should do pretty well. That means keeping them informed of major decisions that will affect their working lives, from pay to job security. That means giving them extra breaks on those days when the heat taps 95 degrees for the third day in a row and also supplying plenty of cold water. That also means insisting that work sites be carefully prepared and maintained with an eye towards safety as well as overall efficiency.

Add in some tool reimbursements and maybe even a small power-tool replacement program. Buy a cordless drill to replace the personally owned drill a carpenter wore out, and you may draw an amazed stare, but also some quiet gratitude. Recognize excellence with raises, of course, but also with praise. Praise really does help, assuming it is sincere. Empty praise works about as well as empty canteens in the desert.

Firings

None of us want to deal with this. We've all been there. If you've never been fired, then you are among a tiny minority. It can be a destructive experience, but it can also help someone make some useful changes in life.

Firing needs to be done in as calm, direct, and coherent a manner as possible. Before you fire someone, you need to provide the employee with at least one written warning, noting what the problems are and suggesting they be corrected. If you don't, your unemployment insurance premiums will go up, because the firing may be classed as unjustified. The warnings and written company policy about grounds for firing help to prevent claims of unjustified firing.

Plan ahead by including in your company policy, in writing, what you consider grounds for firing. Supply this to each person you hire as part of the paperwork they're to read, keep, and occasionally check. Generally, valid firings are violations of company policy, such as continued lateness to work, especially after repeated warnings, repeated inattention to safety rules, and repeated early departures from work without permission. Other valid reasons are deteriorating performance on a long-term basis, with no effort made to correct the decline.

Fired employees are not eligible for unemployment insurance. Employees that are laid off when work slacks off are eligible for unemployment benefits.

If your crew has a lead carpenter, you may also want to check with him or her to make sure you're not acting rashly. It does happen.

When firing an employee, do it at the end of the workday, and have the final paycheck already cut and ready. Depending on your policy, you may wish to add some severance pay. Whether or not you discuss the reasons again with the employee is up to you, but remember that discussion is apt to lead to venting, and you may well need to sit hard on your own temper. If at all possible, make the parting as cordial as possible.

Once you've established your employment procedures and hired your crew, you need to go about getting it in shape and working to your standards on your schedule.

Time will tell you the best mix and size for your crew people, from apprentices to leads to journey levels. Eventually, you may wish to run more than a single crew. You yourself may change from hands-on work to working as your own lead or even total supervisory work and management. After you find the right people and sort out the mixes, you can then work several jobs at one time.

Do it right, though, even if you're only hiring a single apprentice-level helper for a week's work. Get the person who you believe will work best with you. And continue to get the employees who will work best with you, or with your crews, and your home-based carpentry business can step closer to full-time prosperity.

CHAPTER EIGHT

CABINETRY AND CUSTOM FURNITURE

For the first year or two, any carpentry business, whether involved with remodeling or some form of new construction, may have trouble keeping a steady flow of work through the colder months. This presents problems in holding a work team together, as well as in keeping cash flow on a sane and sensible basis. The consistent bane of small businesses is cash flow. Building your business to where cash flows when you need it to flow is a chore harder than constructing the most complex residence, and may take several years. Keeping up some cash flow during the winter months is difficult unless you've managed to plan indoor work in several structures. Even after you've been in business for some time, such planning doesn't always succeed.

Thus there's a need for a form of business related to carpentry to carry some people through the cold, cold days. Here's where skills in cabinetmaking and custom furniture building can be a big help. The profit margins on cabinets may not seem as good as those on construction jobs, but if cabinetry is to be a source only of winter income, profit is somewhat less important, as it only needs to be sufficient to keep things rolling until the building season is under way again. At the same time, it's nice to make a decent buck year-round, instead of for just half to three-quarters of the year, so keeping profit margins reasonable makes sense.

In switching from general carpentry, no matter how precise, to at least part-time cabinet installation and cabinetmaking, you will need more space for work. This space can be in or around your home, or in a shop area elsewhere that you've bought or rented. You will almost certainly need a different array of tools, as well as the skills to operate those tools well enough to satisfy customers. If you do only installations, you must still use tools designed for finish work, so the old circular saw is going to get far less use and your table saw will get far more wear and tear. At this point, those two-hundred-dollar table saws show their weaknesses badly.

If you don't have cabinetry skills, you must gain them before you can do the work, and often, carpentry and cabinetry skills aren't readily come by at the same time. There are a number of ways to gain such skills, starting with experience in local cabinet shops, extending to local work-study options, and going on to a study of wood technology in schools such as Berea College, in Berea, Kentucky. How you gain the skill to produce either cabinetry or furniture is less important than the simple fact that it isn't wise to begin such a business, even as a cold-weather supplement to a carpentry business, without being certain you can produce what you sell.

At the outset, you need to define just what you mean by cabinetry or custom furniture. I have one friend who makes as much as 50 percent of his gross income building simple furniture, usually lawn furniture. He turns out his own versions, developed over many years, of Adirondack chairs, love seats, tables, and various kinds of picnic tables. He does other work, too: gun cabinets, a solid walnut corner cabinet with raised panel door construction, heaven only knows how many fancy mailboxes and posts, a cedar bedroom suite, several entertainment center cabinets, and a podium stand for a teacher.

There are several ways to go about working with cabinets and custom furniture, including a couple that do not involve actual cabinetmaking. The installation of ready-made cabinets, whether from a custom manufacturer or from one who makes only stock models, is a great way to work your way through winters and to supplement other kinds of remodeling jobs. Such work tends to involve extensive kitchen and bathroom remodeling, as does much of cabinetmaking, but the plumbing and wiring work can be covered by your usual subs, who may well be happy to find extra work during the off months.

Working with furniture requires even more complex skills than cabinetmaking in some areas, and may require even more tools (lathe, shaper, etc.). In this chapter, we'll discuss some of the most commonly needed tool upgrades for cabinet and furniture work, give a few tips on setting up your space, and take a general look at how much more complicated the tool situation may make your life.

WORKING IT OUT

Do a quick reexamination of your resources before getting involved in cabinetry, because even the mildest form of this work will take up more space and might create conflicts with zoning laws. Even for fairly simple cabinet installation, you'll usually find a need for a larger, enclosed truck to protect cabinets from the weather. Parking that truck in a residential area may cause problems. If you have already gotten a variance for the other trucks you're running, this one is taken care of, and worries are fewer.

The work space you need may depend on the type of work you are doing. If you emphasize bookcases, for example, you may find yourself doing a lot of built-in work with materials no wider than a foot (except for the backing boards). But if you're building cabinets for entire kitchens, that takes space. Remember that sheet goods at least 4 feet by 8 feet make up most of the material that goes into today's cabinets. Those 32-square-foot sheets of plywood and MDF and laminate require both storage space and a considerable amount of working room. As an example, any table saw used to cut such panels needs some form of run-out guide, and a wide fence, usually to the right of the blade. Of course, both the roller guides and the fence add to the cost of the saw, but the fact is that the bigger problem is the space needed. While tool arrangement can help minimize space needs, you must consider the basics of feeding the saw, which means about 10 feet of space in front of the saw, and of running material off the end, which means at least 8 feet of space past the end of the saw blade. Cuts to the right are often made 50 inches wide, and require about 5 feet more space to the right of the blade.

Consider zoning once more, assuming you're using those tools in or near your home. Your neighbors may show a distinct lack of fondness for the moneymaking whine of saws and other tools, particularly if you're not careful about the hours you work. If there are possible zoning conflicts, irritating the neighbors is a great way to bring the problem to a head.

Consider some form of soundproofing, and try to confine your work to more or less normal business hours. I've got a friend who cannot understand why people living next to homes he remodels consistently get upset when he starts at, or before, first light. Don didn't seem to understand that the shriek of a circular saw isn't music to the ears of the average citizen at 5:00 A.M., but after more than thirty years in the business, he's working in towns more, and is beginning to get the drift. If you irritate people, you lose customers and create needless hassles.

TABLE SAWS

The table-saw variations available today are far greater than ever before, combining some effects of technology along with the simpler, but no less important, directives of many years of experience. The possibilities range from a 10-inch bench-top table saw that weighs under 50 pounds to huge 12-inch blade models that weigh well over ten times that much. Along the way, there's a table saw for almost everyone who needs one in a cabinet shop application. Start by evaluating how much cutting you'll be doing, and how accurate those cuts must be. Remember that work in hardwoods over ¾-inch thick, and extensive work in MDF and hardwood plywoods, requires more power and greater saw stability.

Regardless of what is said by many so-called experts, wood is best worked to within a sixty-fourth of an inch, and not in microns or in thousandths of an inch. Thus you need, at most, a saw that will work to within a sixty-fourth of an inch for greatest accuracy, and one that will repeat such accuracy as often as you need it to. That is where the differences fall: repeatability over time. If you're only going to make one or two dozen cuts a week, with required accuracy limited to a thirty-second of an inch, or even a sixteenth of an inch, then the cheapest lightweight saws are all you need until project requirements change. You'll want a better saw if you needs are in a middle range, with repeatability of a thirty-second of an inch and a hundred or so cuts weekly most of the time, with the occasional project requiring a full sixty-fourth-inch accuracy.

If you need is hundreds or thousands of cuts weekly, week after week after week, within a sixty-fourth of an inch, and you wish for even greater accuracy, you have a smaller and more costly selection of saws from which to choose. But you still have a selection. You can wish all you want for greater accuracy, but the fact is that the medium of wood does not readily provide finer precision on a consistent basis.

The basic bench-top saw has improved greatly in the past year or two. Three with which I have direct experience come from Skil, Black & Decker, and Ryobi. These saws present a good solution for the very basic cabinetmaking shop, where little custom work is done, but they are woefully underpowered and low on accuracy for other uses. The price is right, with prices unlikely to rise above $200. (The Ryobi BT3000 is considerably more expensive, but offers more, while remaining underpowered and somewhat suspect in durability.) All have 10-inch blades, and reasonable accuracy within limits. None have the capacity to take larger fence systems (Ryobi already has a fancy installed fence system). And they're not particularly well suited to larger shop-built accessories such as sliding miter tables. But they'll fill the bill for the first category of basic bench-top table saws, at a reasonable cost, and will endure a good amount of use without losing their basic accuracy. With these saws, figure on an accuracy to within about a thirty-second of an inch, with durability extending over a few dozen cuts per week.

I like to have one or more of these inexpensive saws on hand for times when the standard shop saw is locked up on other jobs. And it's handy to have a relatively low-cost tool set to one side of the shop with a dado head in place, so that specialty cuts may be made without breaking down the setup on the big saw. In fact, at today's low prices, the serious cabinetmaker might think about having two of these saws ready, one with dado blade in place and one with a molding head.

Stepping up one pace, we find the wide variety of Craftsman table saws from Sears. Saws similar to the Craftsman models come from Powermatic, Delta, Grizzly, Jet, and other makers. I have wide experience with Craftsman saws, decent experience with the Makita, and recent experience with the Ryobi BT3000.

Craftsman models present open-work side tables. Some people say the grids in these tables need filling, as you're likely to catch your fingers in them. I've used many saws with these grids, and I've never knocked a finger or scraped a knuckle. Like everything else in a woodworking shop, use of this tool requires some thought, and you will find that dragging your fingers along a table saw's table, with or without an open-work grid, is not really a good work habit.

We come now to my basic complaint about lighter-weight table saws: The blasted table inserts all require operations for change. In most cases, you must back out, and remove one or two screws—which can easily be lost in the piles of sawdust at the table saw. Such operations are also time wasters. Nothing beats the insert system on Delta's Unisaw. (This saw is discussed in the next section.) The Unisaw insert just drops in place. All others should, but that will require the inserts to be made thicker and better fitting, and the insertion space to be cut more deeply and precisely.

It's a lazy man's complaint, I guess, but I find the Unisaw insert is also easier to level with the table surface and less likely to tilt up on one end and down on the other. Also, the insert is heavy enough that it is never going to warp or twist, a problem with some less costly saws.

Light Production Saws

The next level of table saws is the light production model. The Delta entry in the field is the Unisaw, and it more or less sets the standard, as it has for decades. These saws are definitely not portable. Once set up, they are best left in place, as their exceptional accuracy is better maintained when the saw isn't jerked around. The Unisaw weighs in at about 400 pounds in its most basic form, and each step up in equipment carries more weight. Motor covers are not standard equipment on the Unisaws, but other features are far more important. The miter slot is a T slot (with the horizontal slot on the bottom), so the miter gauge is held more accurately. There is a magnetic motor starter available—and I recommend it, as it keeps the motor from restarting without permission if power is cut off from any place other than the switch. The trunnions that hold the unit together are truly massive, and rack and worm gears elevate and tilt the blade mechanism. Power? It's pretty much up to you, but the standard power is a 1⅛-horsepower motor. There is also a 3-horse motor, 220 volt only. The 1½-horse plug to bring it down to 110.

For factories, there's a 5-horse three-phase Unisaw unit, but in my unabashed opinion, three-phase power has no place in the home shop. It is too complex—if you don't believe that, get three industrial electricians or electrical engineers talking about it. The overall confusion and expense elevate things to an industrial level very quickly. I remark on this in part because there is a continuing temptation to buy discarded tools from industry and school sources. Such tools are sold long before their useful life is over, but almost all are for three-phase power—not really a good buy unless you've got a very low-cost source of electrical motors of the right frame types.

Delta is not the only maker of light production table saws. The list is longer than it used to be, with the addition of models from Jet, Grizzly, and others. Powermatic has always provided a superb saw that is strong competition for the Unisaw. A Canadian company, General Manufacturing, turns out a lovely version of the 10-inch tilting arbor table saw.

Powermatic saws usually cost a touch more than the Delta products (about 5 to 10 percent more), but may offer an extra feature or two. Quality is on a par with the Unisaw (and both companies will be angry at that statement because both have a great deal of deserved pride of product).

General Manufacturing matches the pride of product, and the features, but presents a few problems with pricing. I have given up trying to figure Canadian pricing, and distribution tends to be a bit iffy outside the northeastern United States. The saw is worth it if you can find one; price premium tends to be about 10 percent.

The Taiwanese saws, such as the Jet and the Grizzly, present most, and often all, of the features offered by Delta, Powermatic, and General Manufacturing, but at a lower price, and a slightly lower quality level. The recent appearance and feel of the Jet cabinet saw, however, speaks well of its quality, though it still must stand the test of time.

It is not just labor that is cheaper in the countries that produce lower-cost tools. In general (and like all generalized statements, this one is not always true), the gray cast iron used is of lesser quality and treatment. Machining may also be less accurate.

The point of import saws is a simple one: You get a great deal of tool for the money. The cost is about two-thirds that of an equivalent-size American model. The Jet sells for about four-fifths the price of the Unisaw. The downside on the import saws is that you must spend extra hours getting the setup just on and making sure the tool is accurate across a broad range. The three North American brands can usually be taken from a shipping carton and put to work, though I'd recommend a complete check of all nuts, bolts, belts, and so on. The imports need for long-term work-up for complete accuracy is also true of the lower-cost American-made tools. I've known people who spent upwards of a year doing off-and-on fiddling with a Craftsman band saw to get it cutting properly. Delta's units are just about spot-on as delivered.

Radial-Arm Saws

Back in 1922, when Ray DeWalt invented the radial-arm saw, there was no electronic wizardry, nor was there much beauty, but the saw did the work for which DeWalt intended it. In recent years, Black & Decker has transferred the DeWalt name to its line of high-quality portable power tools and dropped radial-arm saws completely. That leaves fewer makers, principally Delta, Sears Craftsman, and Ryobi.

The basic advantage of the radial-arm saw comes in cross-cutting. It will rip, but it is not as safe or accurate in rip work as the table saw. I've reached the stage in my life where I will *not* do rip work on a radial-arm saw.

Many of today's radial-arm saws also accept router bits on an accessory shaft, and of course they do all sorts of dadoing and similar work, with the cut actually visible to the operator. Table saws do the same work, but the cut isn't visible until it is finished, which tends to complicate setup a little bit. Radial-arm saws also shine brightly when squaring up the ends of long stock and when making miter and bevel and compound crosscuts in long stock. Placed correctly, the radial-arm saw has no limits on the length of the material it can cut. In practical circumstances, it isn't all that difficult to make sure you can trim either end of a 16-foot-long board, about the longest standard length you're going to find today.

At one time, the radial-arm saw was touted by some experts as the perfect saw for the one-saw shop. It isn't, never was, and couldn't be, but then no saw is.

Radial-arm saws can be finicky to tune and to keep in tune, so that needs to be kept in mind when selecting one for a shop. I would not use a radial-arm saw as a basic saw. It is a superb supplementary cabinetmaker's tool that can do a great many things more easily than can a table saw or a band saw, but it is not a replacement for a table saw and most certainly will not replace a band saw. With some quick adjustments and a few accessories, the table saw—basically a ripsawing machine—can be made into a superb cut-off machine as well, but it is never going to be truly fantastic, except with a sliding table, at making miter cuts.

The table saw and the band saw are the two primary tools for a cabinetmaking shop. You can fairly easily live without the radial-arm saw. But if you get one, I recommend nothing less than the new 12-inch Delta (or larger), which is going to run about $1,600, or an old, old DeWalt, which can run $3,000 and up.

Other tools are essential, and Ryobi's new woodworking system drill press, with its 18½-inch capacity, is an excellent addition. You need something to drill accurate holes for all those shelf supports, and the Ryobi does the job.

FLOOR SPACE

The amount of floor space needed will differ from person to person. I'm something of a klutz, so I like to have wide aisles and plenty of stumbling room elsewhere. Other people work well in a tightly fitted shop and feel uncomfortable with spaces not filled with tools or materials or storage. Still, any opening between tools, and between tools and benches, needs to be at least 30 inches wide. A table saw needs a 10-foot lead-in and about 2 feet less for materials run-out. If you do a lot of long work, feed the table saw out over a workbench with its height adjusted to accept that run-out; you can then use the bench for other things when no one is using the saw.

Overlap is an important consideration in saving space in shops where only a few people are working. You need to figure out which tool spaces can profitably (from a standpoint of safety, work efficiency, and space efficiency) be overlapped and which cannot.

If you overlap the feeds for a table saw and a planer in one direction, all may work well, but if you do it in the other direction, problems may crop up. Basically, the planer may feed into the front of the table saw after at least 8 feet of run-out space, but it is probably best not set to run into the table saw from the rear. The planer can overlap its feed with the table saw from the sides, of course, with the table-saw blade down and rip fence removed; the saw table then serves as a handy helper. Placing a planer so that its out-feed table runs the finished stock over a table-saw table depends on two things: First, the tables must be close to the same height (with the table saw lower than the planer, if there is a difference); second, you must set up so that chips and dust from the planer do not foul the table saw. The planer turns out more waste in the form of chips and dust than does any other tool, a fact that always needs consideration. If you do much cabinet work, sooner or later you're going to want a planer.

Planers and table saws do best placed near the main entry door or doors, because they are the machines you're most likely going to be feeding long stock into frequently. By making it easy to get the stock to the tool, you save time and energy, thus creating a shop where you rush less and don't get to tired. Taking one's time and being well rested are foundation stones of workshop safety.

Using planned in-feed and out-feed overlaps, you can design a shop with many tools, and relatively small space needs. A very good friend of mine, Bobby Weaver, has all his table saws feed onto workbenches built at exactly the same height as the saw tables (which are placed on stands Bobby designed and built). He has four table saws, an unlikely number for a small shop, but all get used.

No matter what size shop you create, there is a need for some space saving. Even if you could afford to construct an aircraft hangar, you'd eventually fill it. Check all sizes of your tools, and of the tools you plan to buy. Draw a diagram on quarter-inch graph paper close to scale, and make cardboard cut-outs of the tools and their placements. It's probably best, on major stationary tools such as planer, table saw, jointer, and band saw, to make the cut-out big enough to include the in-feed and out-feed needs of the tool (run-in, run-out).

Most band saws have considerably higher tables than do table saws, scroll saws, sanders, and so on, so are easily place close to benches at the rear, and possibly one side, as long as there's sufficient working room for the operator.

Leave yourself enough free space to concentrate on doing your work safely, regardless of which tool you're placing. It pays off in better work, and in fewer nicks, cuts, and missing digits. Don't waste space, though, for too much space between tools can be almost as bad as too little. You can run yourself ragged getting wood from one station to another in such cases.

Try to envision your work habits, based on the projects you now build and those you intend to build. If you start with raw wood, you want a protected area to store the drying wood, and an even better-protected area to store wood that's finished drying. You want easy transfer from the first to the second, or to a vehicle if it is to be taken and kiln dried after air drying. The stack of seasoned wood needs to be close by the door that leads directly to your planer. From there, you'll want to go to a radial-arm saw (possibly), or a power miter saw, to cut the wood to length. After than, you need a jointer and, only then, a table saw. Beyond the table saw, or beside it, you want your drill press and band saw. If you do a lot of lathe work, that needs to be near the table saw, but probably beyond a gluing bench where you might glue up section of countertops.

Finally, there's the finish area. Most small cabinetry shops are, and will remain, light in the finishing area. Finish is stored under a bench, and brushes are kept covered under the same bench. Everything is brushed or blown clean before finishing is started, and the entire shop has to cease work on other projects when one is drying.

Much depends on whether or not you use spray equipment. While spraying finishes gives the smoothest and best coverage, it isn't suitable for all projects. Thus, investing in air compression gear and spray guns becomes iffy for many of us. We're not talking a new hammer here. A good air compressor and tank and spray equipment is going to cost several hundred dollars and eat some shop space.

HVLP spray equipment is more compact, easier to use, and wastes less material. But the good basic units start at about 500 bucks, and the curve is sharply upward after that. I find them invaluable, but many others don't use them at all, never have, and don't miss then (or at least they think they don't miss them).

Your finish area may need some enclosure to protect it from dust and to protect other areas from over-spray and fumes. If you enclose your area, use a spark-free fan to exhaust air to the outside.

In most small shops, spraying is moderate, and special venting may not be needed. Good shop ventilation is a requirement anyway, with the few windows placed to give good cross-ventilation.

STORAGE

If you build cabinets from scratch, some form of wood storage is essential, with the size depending on operation size and style. Starting from raw wood creates greater storage needs and demands more tools (planer, jointer), but provides total control. Plywood needs a lot of storage room, and all wood must be protected from dampness.

Plan for wood storage, for the most part, outside your shop. Keeping a few hundred board feet of lumber inside the shop is a good idea, as is keeping a dozen or so sheets or your most frequently used plywood immediately on hand, along with a bin of scraps. But storing a large lumber supply indoors can create many problems. Even the massive cabinet and furniture shops in this area don't store more than a few days' supply indoors. It eats space, for one thing, and tends to carry some passengers as it is brought in, including various insects, plus general woodsy debris such as grass stems and heads.

Construct a shed to keep the weather off wood supplies that aren't stored in the shop, or use a tarp or section of metal roof to cover the pile. Make sure the layers or any outdoor pile of boards are separated with dry ¾-inch by ¾-inch sticks that run the full width of the stack and are placed every 2 feet along each layer. Keep the first layer up off the ground at least 6 inches.

Do not ever use lightweight woven poly tarps for wood storage. First, the tarps transfer color when whipped by the wind, so they're not much general use in keeping wood clean. Second, and worse, the tarps do not stand weather well, and deteriorate to the point of leaking within a short period of time; often as little as three weeks. They're cheap, and worth less than they cost.

BASIC CABINETMAKING NEEDS

For the most part, your basic cabinetmaking needs are met out of your current toolbox, but you must upgrade the table saw or (preferably) add a light production saw to your contractor's saw, and add more storage and work space at or around your home office. A precision drilling tool of some kind is an absolute essential. Hand drills just don't hack it. If you work up to furniture building, expect to need a planer, jointer, and lathe. The first two are also going to be essential if you work with solid wood cabinets or facings.

A minimum shop size for table saw, drill press, planer, and jointer is 12 feet by 20 feet, and that really is cutting it close, leaving room for two very considerate people to work together. Twice that width and double the length will provide storage, plus room for the lathe, a band saw, and the multitude of other tools you'll soon need.

You'll choke a bit when you see the prices on light production machinery (a Unisaw runs from two to three times the price of a contractor's saw), but all is not lost. Shop around, looking for used machinery, and you can save a lot of money. Unisaws, Powermatic's model 66, and similar tools seldom truly wear out in any appreciable way, so buying used, even machines thirty and forty years old or more, makes sense. Designs haven't changed much, and durability is incredible, so a tool that has been cared for halfway sensibly is apt to be a great buy at anywhere up to half of today's retail price. All in all, you should be able to set up the operation, exclusive of materials and space, for less than $5,000.

TOOLS FOR CABINETMAKING AND FURNITURE BUILDING

Tools	Space Needs	Cost
Table saw. You must upgrade to a more accurate, durable model that holds precise settings.	Variable, according to layout, but generally at least 16' long and 6' wide.	$750 (used) to $3,000.
Drill press. A floor model is preferable to a benchtop model. Ryobi's drilling system is a good one, as are some of the radial-head models.	Depends on work length. Access of 8' on each side is handy; may be over any other tool not apt to be in use at the same time.	From about $450 to $70.
Planer. For most light operations, a 12" portable planer does nicely, and cost tends to be reasonable. Larger planers get costly.	In-feed of at least 8', with a similar-length out-feed. Overall width from 24" to 36", depending on planer width.	Portable 12" planers from $00 to about $650; stationary 12" and wider planers from $1,000 to $4,000.
Jointer. A stationary 6" long bed (60") jointer is almost essential for accurately planed wood edges—which are essential to good wood joints.	In-feed needs 6', and out-feed the same. Overall width about 2'.	From about $550 to $1,400.
Sprayer. A good grade of HVLP finish sprayer is eventually going to be needed. I'm impressed with the Campbell-Hausfield commercial HVLP unit. It is on the low end of the price scale.	Clean area where projects can be protected from dust. Varies according to cabinet or furniture size (or entire shop can be shut down for finishing).	$500 to about $1,000 for a single-gun unit.
Space. Whew. You figure this and you figure the cost.	Space needs never stop, and are always larger than what is available.	As a builder, you can save money whether converting or building new.

CHAPTER NINE

THE ART OF ESTIMATING

kill in estimating for bidding is all-important to the success of a builder. With good estimates, you're bound to make a living. With poor estimates, you'll go broke with great speed. All the other possible problems of the start-up carpentry business fade before problems with estimates: Your estimating skills must be excellent, or you will fail. Do it wrong once, and you may survive. Do it wrong twice, and you won't.

Your estimates should include the cost of materials and labor, tools, and incidentals. You then figure in an already determined percentage as your profit, and present the bid. If the bid is low enough to be reasonable, you will get the job. You then have to complete it as stated in the bid or within a few percentage points of your estimate. By law, you cannot exceed your estimate by more than 10 percent, unless specific conditions that change the estimate are present.

SETTING UP TO MAKE YOUR ESTIMATES

When you begin with small jobs, estimates are far simpler and easier than they will be when you work with a crew and with subcontractors. Your crew members are soon known factors to you and estimating their labor isn't a problem for long. You hope your subs are known factors, especially since they have to present you with estimates, and your overall job estimate depends on their reliability and thus affects your profit. Small jobs usually mean lost time due to goofs in estimating or failure to thoroughly check out subsurface problems. I recall a remodeling job for which I had to remove knotty-pine paneling from a living-room wall, which had a bathroom on the other side, and re-cover the wall with Sheetrock, which was to be painted. No big deal. I pulled the knotty-pine paneling and discovered the wall was not attached to floor, ceiling, or wall framing at its junction. That meant the wall did its level best to fall on me, though it was restrained by a toilet hanger and a wall-hung lavatory in the bathroom. I ended up having to make a few changes not covered in the estimate and split the difference with the homeowner, who had no idea the wall was like that. To this day, I wonder just how the original builder ever got that knotty pine nailed to the studs.

Make a list of things you need to do to make accurate estimates. The basic tools for making estimates are simple things, including a 50-foot or 100-foot tape measure, an adding machine (or calculator or computer), a legal-size pad or two, and a set of the job plans for everyone who needs a set, including all your subcontractors.

Set up a folder. I like to use those large, red envelopes with a wide expansion gullet and a big flap. They come with a little ribbon to hold things together, and among the first things I do is toss the ribbon and use a big rubber band. Things don't drop out of this setup as easily as they do a regular file folder. You can file the envelope or carry it with you. If you use a regular file folder, use at least two big rubber bands to keep it shut.

Start by making sure you've got all the telephone numbers you are going to need, beginning with your customer's numbers. If there is an architect or designer on the job, you'll need that number, and you will need the local building inspector's number. There may be others; if you expect to have to call a person more than once during a job, make a record of that person's telephone number.

At this point, I cannot see anything to recommend the little hand-held computers called PDAs. These are personal digital assistants and to date each and every one is bug-ridden and expensive. When the concept finally works, it will be great, but now it's just a $900 piece of trash, regardless of the brand. For the PDA to work, it needs a much better recognition factor for handwriting, and, of course, that's where the big problem lies. Many of us can't read our own handwriting after a few weeks, a point to keep in mind when making notes for your files.

Don't file alphabetically unless you like confusion. Set your notes and quotes files in the order in which the job is going to be done. If the framing crew is first, all figures and information related to framing is first in your file. Then add in your paperwork on the electrical sub, plumbing sub, insulation sub, drywall sub, painting sub, and finish carpentry crew. If you're doing all site prep and then working from the excavation up, set the files up in that order and carry out your estimating procedure in that order, making sure you miss no steps.

EXPERIENCE COUNTS

An efficient setup for estimating is nice to use, saves time, and usually increases accuracy, but the most valuable estimating tool on-site is your experience. It is not the experience of a subcontractor, or the architect, or anyone else. Sure, a sub can save you a ton of money by suggesting faster, simpler, better ways to do his or her jobs when you have trouble visualizing methods. But that's part of the sub's job. You need to bring together all the disparate elements of the job, from excavation to topping out, meld them into one unit, and produce an estimate that gets you the job . . . and makes you a decent profit. Thus, experience is an essential.

As we've gone through various topics in this book, my assumption has been that you've had experience as a journey-level carpenter, then as a lead carpenter, and finally as a subcontractor in some areas. If I had no other way of getting experience as a sub, I'd hire myself out to one of the house-building outfits that build hundreds of houses a year, working exclusively with subcontractor crews. (Their own people serve as site managers.)

Working, for example, as a framing sub on thirty jobs in one season is going to really hone your skills at speccing the framing areas of a job. You may want to work a bunch of jobs as a finish carpenter sub for such an outfit before you get into business for yourself. Most prime contractors who start as carpenters work as frame-and-finish carpenters on their own jobs. Knowing it from thirty or more jobs instead of half a dozen, as is more likely to be the case with most of us, is much better.

Work Estimate

Date

Nail & Screw Builders

Estimate good for 30 days
unless otherwise noted

Job Description:

_____

_____

_____

_____

Itemized Estimate

Total	

This estimate applies only to the job described above. This estimate does not include additional materials or labor that may be required due to any unforeseen problems that arise once the job has begun.

WORKING FROM PLANS

Working from measurements and plans is essential to good estimating. Having clear plans on hand is a big help, but not always possible. Many smaller remodeling jobs and, for that matter, many small building jobs, involve stating a size, finished look, and stage of completion, from which you must make an estimate. Decks are often built, for example, from a description or a photo, and usually work just fine . . . if everything is spelled out in the contract.

I don't know if it's a good idea to measure the linear footage of a one-story building and then class it as needing an equal number of two-by-four studs. I do know some carpenters who estimate that way as long as the wall is 16 inches on-center and doesn't have a lot of extra convolutions. The specs presumably include all studs, both top plates and the sole plate. It seems to work for them, but creates end-wall problems for me, forcing me to figure gables in extra (they're where all the work is, anyway). However you finally decide to work things out, make notes of how you are doing it, what the results are, and any other pertinent information. Do not depend on your mental files. Keep careful notes, and file all the notes as always, in order of the work being done.

Larger jobs must have plans, for otherwise you simply cannot estimate needed materials and time to completion. Can you imagine trying to build a house specced as 64 by 28 feet, with two and a half baths, country kitchen, formal dining room, and three bedrooms, on a slab? Sure. Some discussion of type of slab starts things off, and from there, you move to framing type (two by four or two by six); insulation thickness and type; siding and roofing; type of heat; type and number of fixtures; type of electrical service; number and type and placement of receptacles; and a host of other features.

Even with good measurements taken from good, professionally done plans, you cannot build a house without a careful site inspection.

SITE CONDITIONS AFFECT WORKING NEEDS

Site conditions can create or ease problems. A tight site sometimes makes it impossible for trades to work side by side, while poor access to the site slows down materials delivery. Such problems can reduce the speed of all trades to a crawl, sometimes adding 50 percent to the time needed to complete a job.

Site hazards are another story, and one that needs much thought. Around here, open ditches seem to be the major hazard, but there are also some steep areas up in the mountains and near some of the lakes. Other site hazards can be such things as power lines swinging in close to working areas, ponds close to working areas, swampy areas around the site, and even landscape plants that must be protected or avoided. Anything that must be avoided or protected creates time problems and must be figured into your estimate. The same holds true, and more so, for remodeling, when you may be dealing with dust problems for the rest of an occupied dwelling or problems with furniture or fixtures that cannot practically be removed while you work.

AVOIDING PITFALLS

You must know enough to prevent pitfalls with your subs. Some jobs may be done by subs, but may also be considered the responsibility of the prime contractor, you. Who flashes the chimney, for example? That can be readily done when the roof is sheathed and so may be your responsibility, though many roofing subs will do it. On some jobs, you may have a sheet-metal sub who will do the work. Who sets the blocks for shower pipe and for plumbing in general? If you know fixture types and sizes, you can do so when framing out, but many plumbers prefer to do their own. The same with electrical boxes: Electricians may set them or you may, but some electrical contractors have a preference and a reason for that preference. All of this can be worked out when the subs come to the job site to pick up their plan sets.

On extensive jobs, set aside time for each sub and go over job plans and discuss problems that might arise, before he or she works out an estimates, which must then be added to yours. Your profit depends on the accuracy of the estimates you get from your subs, so working with them to get good estimates and ensure the job runs as smoothly as possible is an excellent idea, even if it means a little more give on your part.

PRICING MATERIALS

To produce accurate estimates, you need experience getting correct, up-to-date prices from your suppliers. You need to be able to figure out, from experience, measurements, and plans, what materials are needed. Then you need to know where to get them and what the materials are going to cost. The latter may be the hardest part to calculate in this day of jumpy prices, but getting an accurate price structure for materials is essential, as is getting good delivery schedules from your suppliers.

MATERIALS DELIVERY

Getting materials there days before your crew arrives, or days afterward, helps not at all. Every hour your crew spends waiting for materials is lost money. Every hour materials spend out in the weather, with no protection, is lost money. Avoid either by using your experience with suppliers to get the one with the best prices (not always the lowest) and the most accurate delivery schedules.

CHECKLISTS AND WORKSHEETS

Checklists and worksheets take time to develop, and each builder tends to prefer his or her own. The ones I provide here are meant as nothing more than starting points and are not all-inclusive. I've developed these lists on my computer, but they can be done with a lined pad and a ruler, though the computer-designed checklist looks neater and impresses customers, which makes it a good marketing tool.

Some omissions are deliberate. For example, I've left out parking fees because I live in a rural area and don't pay to park at or near a job. Check each list and apply it to your own situations. There are situations that don't often apply to most of the small builders I know, such as installing structural steel or applying stucco, so I've avoided them. I include items for demolition as well as construction because much home-based carpentry work is remodeling, which usually involves the destruction of parts of an area before changes are built.

Around here, excavation is almost always a power job, done by backhoes. Our red clay clings, and can be nearly as hard as concrete in midsummer, when we're short on rain and long on heat. Thus, excavation can be a major expense for full-basement and crawl-space structures, and can be costly even when only footings are poured, at frost depth (18 inches locally).

Contractors also wonder where "two-by" lumber goes much of the time. As a kid, I was told to always add a 10 percent minimum waste allowance. Then my ol' buddy would stare at me, my tools, the sky, and the horizon, before saying "Nah, best make that 15 percent." Waste is waste, and where it goes may be almost anywhere. Generally, it goes into miscuts and wood that gets dropped into mud, or it's wood that kind of slips out the door into the shed next door. With today's lumber quality, some of that 10 percent is going to be in twisted and otherwise deformed pieces, often set in the middle of the pile. I've noted around here, though, that if you buy as a contractor from local building supply houses, you are certain to get better quality materials for your money. The do-it-your-selfer gets nailed when it comes to quality, not the contractor. That creates some problems, but this isn't the place to go into them.

You must allow for waste, but I'd suggest you not list it as waste on your estimates. You may just want to go ahead and add 10 or 15 percent on the harder-to-estimate jobs and not mention it. Some builders call it margin and still end up explaining it to customers. When you tell a customer you're figuring in 10 percent extra on materials for mistakes, miscuts, and miscues, that customer is apt to wonder just what's being built on his or her property. The waste isn't only in two-by lumber, but it often seems so. Check out each job, though, and see if you don't need 5 to 10 percent more in each and every category in which you or your crews do the work. Add that in, for otherwise, you're going to run out.

THE WORLD OF FREE ESTIMATES

I often read on-line notes from builders about charging for estimates and design work. Because nobody wants to waste time and energy doing plans for jobs that never get done or get awarded to others, free estimates are something we'd all probably like to avoid.

Good luck. You *may* be able to charge for estimates in your area, especially, if you are the finest builder in your area and have work lined up for the next two or three years. Otherwise you're going to give free estimates, smile while you're doing them, and even smile when you lose the job due to indecision on the part of the client or to a lower estimate from a lesser builder. Free estimates are a reality in today's competitive market, even though some areas are experiencing building booms.

My recommendation is to make all first estimates free and then charge a reasonable fee for second estimates on the same project. A colleague of mine, who wishes to remain anonymous, provides all estimates free of charge. "I don't do real design work, though I do help lay out a bathroom or kitchen when needed," he said. "Really, the planning work is a sales tool, not a separate way to make money." He does try to keep a strong sense of contact with the prospective client, asking questions about whether or not a second set of specs, a change in design, a change in completion date, a change in any major (and sometimes minor) part of the project might convince the client to accept his bid. Experience has taught him that possible clients often will be reluctant to tell him early in the negotiations that, for whatever reason, they are not really interested in his business. In other words he doesn't learn a prospective client has decided not to do a project or is about to hire someone else until he has done a lot of extra work in an effort to get the job. "We waste salespeople's time because we don't want to turn them down," he says. "Then it happens to us, and we get grumpy. There isn't much to be done about this aspect of human nature, except to keep in as close touch as possible during the bidding process."

Note in the estimating checklists that the word *other* occurs with some frequency. That's because only you and your customers can accurately define your jobs. You may prefer to simply leave half a dozen blank lines in your checklists. Please note, too, that you are not limited to these forms. If your jobs call for different categories, insert them. You can design checklists based on these, use someone else's, or make up your own, but you must have some type of checklist to do an accurate job of estimating.

You also want a summary sheet that lists the totals, and not the specifics, for a final judgment. A model is included near the chapter's end.

ESTIMATING WORKSHEET: DEMOLITION

Demo Type	Labor	Materials	Subcontractor	Total
Bathroom gut				
Kitchen gut				
Room gut				
Finish floor				
Floor frame				
Finish walls				
Wall frame				
Ceiling frame				
Doors				
Roof				
Windows				
Trim				
Porches				
Other				

ESTIMATING WORKSHEET: EXCAVATION

Excavation Type	Labor	Materials	Subcontractor	Total
Site				
Shoring				
Compaction				
Soil treatment				
Finish grade				
Hauling				
Rental equipment				
Other				

ESTIMATING WORKSHEET: CONCRETE

Concrete Work	Labor	Materials	Subcontractor	Total
Staking				
Layout				
Excavate: Hand				
Excavate: Backhoe				
Form stems				
Form walls				
Form stairs				
Form walkways				
Form slabs				
Sand				
Gravel				
Membrane				
Rebar				
Wire				

ESTIMATING WORKSHEET: CONCRETE

Concrete Work	Labor	Materials	Subcontractor	Total
Tie-ins				
Anchor bolts				
Vibrate				
Strip & clean				
Point & patch				
Haul				
Backfill				
Unload and handle				
Other				

ESTIMATING WORKSHEET: DRAINAGE

Drainage Work	Labor	Materials	Subcontractor	Total
Excavate				
Gravel				
Filter cloth				
Drain fabric				
Perf pipe				
Solid pipe				
Other				

ESTIMATING WORKSHEET: FRAMING

Framing Work	Labor	Materials	Subcontractor	Total
Bolts				
Hold-downs				
Joist hangers				
Tie straps				
Nails				
Post bases				
Post caps				
Other fasteners				
Foundation vents				
Rafter vents				
Layout				
Wall frame layout				
Wall frame mudsill				
Walls, cripple studs				
Walls, 2x4				
Walls, 2x6				
Walls, other				
Beams				
Posts				
Headers, door				
Headers, window				
Wall tie-ins				
Plumbing and line				
Ceiling frame layout				
Ceiling ledgers				
Ceiling joists				
Ceiling blocking				

ESTIMATING WORKSHEET: FRAMING

Framing Work	Labor	Materials	Subcontractor	Total
Ceiling tie-ins				
Floor frame layout				
Floor ledgers				
Floor girders				
Floor beams				
Floor joists				
Floor rim joists				
Floor blocking				
Roof frame layout				
Roof ridge				
Roof ledgers				
Roof rafters				
Roof purlins				
Roof collar ties				
Skylights				
Fascia				
Soffit				
Blocking				
Plywood subfloor				
Plywood sheathing				
Plywood roof sheathing				
Furring, drywall				
Blocking, drywall				
Blocking for accessories				
Blocking, miscellaneous				
Other				

ESTIMATING WORKSHEET: EXTERIOR FINISH

Exterior Work	Labor	Materials	Subcontractor	Total
Felt/Tyvek				
Siding				
Siding corner boards				
Rafter tails				
Rafter molding				
Fascia				
Knee braces				
Door casing				
Window casing				
Skirts				
Treads & risers				
Stair rails				
Other				

ESTIMATING WORKSHEET: WINDOWS AND DOORS

Window/Door	Labor	Materials	Subcontractor	Total
Windows				
Skylights				
Greenhouse windows				
Extra hardware				
Caulking				
Flashing				
Prime				
Doors				
Jambs				
Hinges				
Prehang				
Lockset bore				
Hang				
Locksets				
Deadbolts				
Sills				
Threshold				
Closers				
Weatherstrip				
Kick plates				
Push plates				
Other				

ESTIMATING WORKSHEET: INTERIOR STAIRS

Stairs	Labor	Materials	Subcontractor	Total
Stringers				
Skirts				
Risers				
Treads				
Newels				
Posts				
Rails				
Balusters				
Wall rails				
Other				

ESTIMATING WORKSHEET: INTERIOR TRIM

Trim	Labor	Materials	Subcontractor	Total
Hardware				
Nails				
Window sills				
Window stool				
Extensions				
Window apron				
Window jambs				
Window casing				
Door casing				
Base pieces				
Base inside joints				
Base outside joints				
Base footage				
Wall caps				
Stair skirts				
Crown molding pieces				
Crown molding inside joints				
Crown molding outside joints				
Crown molding footage				
Columns				
Closet shelves & poles				
Paneling				
Wainscoting				
Valances				
Bath paper holder				
Towel bars				
Glass shelves				
Grab bars				
Shower rod				
Medicine cabinet				
Other				

ESTIMATING WORKSHEET: CABINETS

Cabinets	Labor	Materials	Subcontractor	Total
Measure site				
Inspect cabinets				
Built-ins				
Vanities				
Kitchen, wall				
Kitchen, base				
Kitchen, full				
Window seats				
Doors				
Pulls				
Other				

ESTIMATING WORKSHEET: DECKS AND FENCES

Decks and Fences	Labor	Materials	Subcontractor	Total
Nails				
Hardware				
Piers				
Other foundation				
Ledgers				
Joists & rim joists				
Decking				
Posts				
Rails				
Stiles				
Fence posts				
Fence rails				
Fence screens				
Nails				
Hardware				
Gates				
Other				

ESTIMATING WORKSHEET: JOB COMPLETION

Completion Work	Labor	Materials	Subcontractor	Total
Caulk				
Drywall touch-up				
Adjust hardware				
Adjust door				
Adjust cabinet				
Repair minor breakage				
Make minor corrections				
Customer instructions				
Other				

JOB ESTIMATE SUMMARY SHEET

Date: _____

Job Address: _____
_____
_____

Project Description: _____
_____
_____
_____
_____
_____
_____
_____
_____
_____
_____
_____
_____
_____
_____
_____
_____
_____
_____
_____
_____
_____
_____
_____

Rough carpentry: _____
Finish carpentry: _____
Subtrades: _____
Contractor's Fee (Markup): _____
Total contractor's charges: _____

LABOR

It matters not whether it's your own labor or that of people you hire. Labor is the hardest part of any job to estimate and is usually the highest cost. I just told my son-in-law to make sure, as he gets estimates for having his roof replaced, that he get the absolute best shingles made, because the labor cost on such a job is at least twice the cost of materials. It's more economical to make sure you never have to do it again, than to save $250 or $350 on shingles. If that much. When labor is even a 50-50 proposition against the cost of materials, you've got to have a good idea of what the crew or your own output will be.

You can get numbers from published manuals, or you can use your past experience as a carpenter and builder, but you've got to have reasonably accurate figures for different jobs and breakdowns of tasks on those different jobs. How long does it take to set forms for a full basement? How long to hang a door, install a sheet of subfloor, or roof, or sidewall sheathing? How long to frame out a stairwell, build basement stairs, or install a window in a rough opening? How long to frame that rough opening? With those figures in hand, you can calculate the total number of work hours for a job.

Not every job is going to allow the same level of productivity from your crews, but the figures will give you a starting point. Your judgment of the job, from the site to the plans, provides the rest of the information. Make any necessary adjustments in the unit cost. For example: Each 32-square-foot sheet of subfloor takes X minutes to install on the average job. The new job requires sixty full sheets and four partials of varying sizes. It also has a lot of unusual floor needs and many openings around stairwells to the basement and other areas. You make allowances but realize too that subflooring takes place before a lot of restrictions are formed with interior room framing, so the actual labor cost increases, other than cutting for partials, is going to be in the finished floor areas. Other considerations might be special underlayments for ceramic tile, and similar needs. Get your adjusted unit cost, and multiply it by sixty, possibly using the four partials as different cases, depending on the complexity of the cuts. A simple cut across the sheet width is not going to add more time than is saved by less nailing, so that comes out even.

Don't forget that there is a thing called labor burden that must be added to your base labor costs when you make your labor estimates. If you're paying someone $15.00 an hour and mandates and benefits add up to $7.50 (Social Security, disability and unemployment insurances, health insurance, pension participation, liability insurance, workmens' compensation, tools and other supplies, and whatever else you offer your employees), your actual labor cost, the base of $15.00 plus the labor burden of $7.50, is $22.50 per hour. Your estimates are going to be pleasantly low if you forget the labor burden, including your own, but you'll also lose money you need to make.

WORKING WITH BUILDING INSPECTORS

Good working relationships are at least as important to a business as any plan or computer program. You can always buy a new program or make a new plan, but damage to a working relationship can be a permanent thing, so you always need to bear those working pals in mind. You need to work with building inspectors, and it's better if your interactions with them are as nonadversarial as possible. I've seen many an overconfident builder run up against a brick wall with a building inspector the builder considers a half-witted bum who works for peanuts. Not a good idea, and not usually true, either. That building inspector decides whether or not your stages pass inspection and whether or not your building job deserves a certificate of occupancy. If you have an honest difference of opinion, present it as such. Trying to shout your opinion down the inspector's throat or threatening the inspector with a call to his boss doesn't often work. My friend Tom is a chief building inspector. He trains his inspectors well, supervises them only as tightly as is essential for good work, and then backs them up all the way. You can believe a loudmouth doesn't dissuade Tom or his inspectors from doing their jobs as they see them. The builder almost always loses, unless things are handled in a sensible manner. If you are absolutely positive the inspector is wrong, try finding and presenting some facts. Getting in the inspector's face is no way to a resolution.

It is a fact that some building inspection departments don't do as well as do others, either at getting work inspected or at protecting the public.

You can help yours along by staying aware of the various codes and building to suit them after you've applied for and received the correct permits.

WHAT YOU ARE GOING TO MAKE: MARKUPS AND WHERE THEY COME FROM

Your markup is not just profit. It must cover your overall expenses beyond materials and labor on a given job, and the list can be a long one, depending on the project and your setup.

Your profit doesn't come until everything else is paid for, and if the payment is too low because of a substandard markup, then your profit is going to be low or nonexistent. Like all capitalists, you need a reward for risking time and money in a business, and profit is that reward. Wages paid to you are not part of that profit.

When you work on a job and manage that job too, you're doing two jobs yourself and need to get paid for both. Thus, if you're paying your lead $20 an hour, figure your time, during hands-on work, at that amount or more. At the same time, you're managing the job, and that pays more, so figure your time as a manager at least a third or more higher than your wage as a carpenter.

All that gets added in to costs, along with lumber, labor for crew, subcontractors, and so on. You then apply your markup to the entire job, working from a fixed percentage, which you need to determine for yourself. You may well feel a need to vary your markup on some jobs, depending on cost and duration.

Your markup needs to bring you a return in line with market rates on similar amounts of money, plus a little. High-risk projects demand higher markups, though keeping crews busy in slack times can justify lower markups simply to keep good crews together. Work it out. Percentages for markup may vary from a low of 6 percent to as much as 16 percent or even more. Remember, that markup comes on top of your salary, so once fixed costs are covered, you see some profit from the markup.

APPENDIX

SOURCES FOR TOOLS AND USEFUL THINGS

Blue Ridge Machinery & Tools, Inc.
Box 536-WSB
Hurricane, WV 25526
(304) 562–3538
Fax (304) 562–5311

The Blue Ridge Machinery catalog of power and hand tools covers a wide range of items, including metal and woodworking machinery, supplies, accessories, books, and videos. Blue Ridge carries tools by Jet, MinMax, Powermatic, and many more companies. Among the tools offered are air compressors, dust collectors, band-saw blades, drill bits, jointers, lathes, planers, routers, sanders, and shapers. The company accepts Discover, Mastercard, and Visa. A catalog costs $1.00.

Blume Supply, Inc.
3316 South Boulevard
Charlotte, NC 28209
(800) 288–9200 or
(704) 523–7811

Blume Supply sells Powermatic and other power tools and provides repairs and rentals. Among the items they list are angle finders, hand saws, rules, squares, utility knives, wrenches, and underhand tools. Blume also handles supplies for woodworkers, including wood buttons, plugs and dowels, glues and screws. Call for prices and other details.

Campbell-Hausfeld
100 Production Drive
Harrison, OH 45030
(800) 634–4793

Campbell-Hausfeld is a leading manufacturer of air compressors, including oilless models. In addition, they have recently come out with a high-volume low-pressure spray kit that is lower in price than industrial versions and works very nicely in applying clear and other finishes in a nonproduction setting. Campbell-Hausfeld also makes a line of compressed-air nailers and staplers for everything from heavy framing to fabric stapling. Their newest design is a round-head-framing nailer, but the preceding one, a lighter-weight stapler, is of more interest to woodworkers. Call and ask for free brochures.

DeVilbiss Air Power Co.
213 Industrial Drive
Jackson, TN 38301
(901) 423–7000
Fax (901) 423–7900

The DeVilbiss line of Air America compressors runs the gamut from a small, three-quarter-horse, oilless model that you can almost tuck in your back pocket to a monster, five-horse two-stage industrial model that delivers 175 psi and weighs 413 pounds. In between, there are Air America models for almost every do-it-yourself or commercial use, with tools to accompany the compressors, such as spray guns, air ratchets, dual-action circular sanders, air-impact wrenches, air chisels, air staplers, jitterbug air sanders, paint tanks, and blow guns. The company is the largest-volume producer of air compressors, and their products are found in many places, including home centers and other retail outlets. Naturally, the compressors will drive finish nailers and similar tools that DeVilbiss now makes. Write for free brochures.

DeWalt Industrial Tool Co.
626 Hanover Pike
Hampstead, MD 21074
(800) 4–DEWALT

The DeWalt Company has been around for more than sixty-five years. Today it sells Black and Decker's top-grade industrial power tools and accessories, aimed primarily at the construction industry. These tools, including the 12-inch compound miter saw, the biscuit joiner, and the big-plunge router, are ideal for serious woodworkers. (They're too pricey for the beginner, but are reasonably priced for tools aimed at surviving the day-to-day battering of construction work.) DeWalt will be glad to supply a catalog of the entire line, which is expanding.

Duluth Trading Co.
P.O. Box 7007
Duluth, MN 55107
(800) 505–8888
(612) 221–0308
Fax (612) 221–0040

Duluth Trading Company is an offshoot of Portable Products, which sells hard goods made in the Lake Superior region. They feature the Bucket Boss and the rest of the Portable Products line in their catalog and also sell Occidental Leather and other tool belts, Gladstone bags—a soft-sided bag with a top that opens to the bag's full width—field bags, a contractor's briefcase (my own personal favorite), a medium duffel bag, and a shell bag and purse, all in green or olive, with leather trim and solid copper and brass hardware. None of this stuff is cheap, but it seems to be fairly priced. The catalog is free for the asking. Duluth Trading Company accepts Discover, Mastercard, and Visa.

Hartville Tool and Supply
940 West Maple Street
Hartville, IN 44632
(800) 345–2396
Fax (216) 877–4682

Hartville is a tool and accessories company. Their full-color catalog is about seventy-five pages long and is issued once or twice annually. The company carries many Porter-Cable tools, some Delta, the InchMate calculator, Dozuki saws, and the DeWalt compound-miter saw. This just skims the list, of course. Hartville accepts Discover, Mastercard, Visa, American Express, and Optima.

Hitachi
3950 Steve Reynolds Boulevard
Norcross, GA 30093
(404) 925–1774
Fax (404) 923–2117

6219 DeSoto Avenue
Woodland Hills, CA 91365
(714) 891–5330
Fax (714) 898–9096

Hitachi tools have been in the U.S. market over a decade now and have earned a reputation for quality. The line consists of more than eighty-five tools for working wood, concrete, metal, and other materials. Of particular interest to builders are the drills, including the cordless models; circular saws, including miter saws with up to 15-inch blades, and a well-regarded slide-compound miter saw; routers; planers; jointer-planers; a 12-inch table saw; and a 14½-inch band saw. The company also produces an exceptionally large line of pneumatic nailers, including finishing and brad nailers that may be of use to many woodworkers. A new U.S. plant, which opened in California in the spring of 1994, aids production and quality control. Hitachi will send along a mini-catalog on request.

International Tool Corp.
1939 Tyler Street
Hollywood, FL 33020
(800) 338–3384
Fax (305) 927–0291

International Tool is a full-line distributor of quality industrial power tools, featuring Porter-Cable, Bosch, Milwaukee, Hitachi, Skil, Ryobi, Delta, DeWalt, Fein, Panasonic, Freud, Senco, Stanley-Bostitch, and many more. After looking through their most recent catalog, I'd have to say that there are few items they don't offer, and their discounts are among the best in the industry. They also manage to cover an awful lot of tools in an eighty-page catalog. This is a must-see catalog if you're in the market for major items and know the tools you're looking for. The catalog, done on newsprint, is free. International Tool accepts American Express, Optima, Mastercard, Visa, and Discover.

Makita U.S.A., Inc.
14930 Northam Street
La Mirada, CA 90638
(714) 522–8088

Makita has recently added 12-volt cordless driver-drills, impact drivers, and hammer-drills to their line of cordless tools. This brings the Makita line of cordless power tools in line with other manufacturers who set 12 volts as the standard for top-of-the line models. Now it's a race to see who will have the hottest 14.4 volt tools before 1996. Also new from Makita is a cordless stapler that drives as many as 750⅝-inch-long staples on a single charge. A random-orbit sander helps round out their line of woodworking sanders, so Makita now has close to a complete line of power tools, including cordless and corded drills, circular saws, miter and compound-miter saws (the Makita 10-inch compound-miter saw is remarkably good), generators, portable planers, electric chainsaws, a 14-inch band-saw, a dust collector, a 12-inch portable planer, a planer-jointer, a couple of table saws, routers, and much more. Among the much more is a modest-width line of gas chainsaws. Call, or write, for dealer's name, and a free full-line brochure (really a catalog).

Milwaukee Electric Tool Corp.
13135 W. Lisbon Road
Brookfield, WI 53005
(414) 781–3600 or
(414) 781–3611

Milwaukee Electric Tool (Canada), Ltd.
755 Progress Avenue
Scarborough, ONT M1H 2W7
(416) 439–4181
Fax (416) 439–6210

Milwaukee has long been one of the leading wide-line electric tool manu-facturers in the country. One of their tools, the Sawzall, has almost become a generic term for a reciprocating saw. Ask a plumber or remodeling con-tractor about a recip saw, and the saw will almost certainly be called the "sawsall." The company has been around a long time (since 1924), and con-tinues to develop professional-level tools for their extensive product line. A recent addition to the line is the 10-inch, 15-ampere Magnum miter saw. There are a lot of other top-quality tools, many of use to woodworkers, including routers, drills, driver-drills, cordless driver-drills, circular saws, grinders, sanders and polishers, random-orbit sanders, heat guns, and a multitude of accessories. The catalog and tool brochures are free.

Nemy Electric Tool Co.
7635-A Auburn Boulevard
Citrus Heights, CA 95610
(916) 723–1088 or
(916) 969–1088
Fax (916) 723–1091

Bill Nemy runs a business founded in 1945 and in its ninth year in its current location. Nemy Electric Tool Company is one of the larger wood-working machinery dealers in northern California. It serves the profes-sional community, hobbyists, wood-carvers, and cottage-industry woodworkers. They also do job-shop work for restoration and antiques dealers, and they repair tools. Nemy offers classes in woodworking, woodcarving, production techniques, stair building, and other skills. He's produced a video on arched raised panels, which is projected as the first of a series of thirteen. The video is eighty-three minutes long and details building raised panels with a router and router table. Nemy's cat-alog is $2.50, and his *Woodworker's Bulletin* newsletter is free. Nemy Elec-tric Tools accepts Discover, Mastercard, and Visa.

Northern Hydraulics
P.O. Box 1219
Burnsville, MN 55378
Orders (800) 533–5545

Northern Hydraulics's free 136-page catalog does have a lot of hydraulic equipment and parts, but there's a strong emphasis on hand and power tools, too. Lines carried include Milwaukee, Bosch, Skil, Makita, Channellock, their own NH, Hirsh, Vise-Grip, Homelite, Campbell-Hausfeld, Black and Decker, DeWalt, Ingersoll-Rand, and most others. Also, if you wish to buy 250-pound-capacity pneumatic 8-inch swiveling casters, this is the only mail-order service I know of. There's a long ton of such stuff, including 1,500-pound industrial-grade casters (I can't even imagine a need for such things, but someone somewhere will). Prices are reasonable, and I've ordered from them often enough to state their shipping times are also reasonable. Northern accepts Mastercard and Visa.

Portable Products, Inc.
58 East Plato Boulevard
St. Paul, MN 55107
(800) 688–2677

This manufacturer of portable products also sells direct. The products are carried by many woodworker's catalogs, and by Sears, K-Mart, Target, Hechingers, Ace, Home Depot, and other outlets. The company is owned and operated by tradesmen. What do they make and sell? The mainstay of the line is the bucket-mounted tool carrier. Having said that, it's necessary to state that there are six versions of that mainstay, plus a bucket seat. (There's also a padded handle for those buckets.) The entire line is meant to be mounted on five-gallon plastic buckets, has many pockets, and is made, in various patterns, of heavy material meant to last a long time under extreme conditions. There is also a folding-top Parachute Bag to hold small parts (nails, screws, and similar items), a lower-priced version of the full-size bag, called Chutes, knee pads in three versions, and suspenders. There is no pretension whatsoever: Tools are tested by tradesmen, and the catalog is very well done. A related company, Duluth Trading Company (listed above), sells retail and carries a wider line of mail-order goods.

Porter-Cable
P.O. Box 2468
Jackson, TN 38302
(800) 4U–STOOL or
(901) 668–8600
Fax (901) 664–0549

Porter-Cable is one of the smaller of the major U.S. tool manufacturers, but it produces a wide line of portable power tools with quality second to none. The company has been around for eighty-eight years. Among their products are circular saws; a laser-guided 10-inch miter saw; routers (up to 3¼-horsepower five-speed monsters, both fixed and plunge); router bits; bayonet saws; the quietest of all biscuit joiners; sanders—belt, orbital, random orbit, and circular; plus several models of the famed Magna quench cordless drill, one of the first 12-volt cordless drills and still one of the most powerful. Their model 550 pocket-cutting kit is probably the best low-cost solution for the small-scale cabinet shop that does a lot of face-frame building. There are also portable band-saws, reciprocating saws, the most complete line of laminate trimmers I have seen, shears and grinders, and polishers. Their line of router bits is among the largest. The new black-oxide finish is durable and reduces rust problems. Write for a copy of their free catalog if your interest in hand-held power tools extends to industrial quality tools over and beyond the above range.

Ryobi American Corp.
P.O. Box 1207
Anderson, SC 29625
(800) 525–2579

Ryobi calls its line of power tools the Workaholics. The company makes a wide variety of products, from printing equipment to hardware and sporting goods. They also produce lightweight aluminum castings for most of their tools. Ryobi makes bench-top tools and portable power tools, including a remarkable oscillating spindle sander, a table saw, a 12-inch planer, and a 9-inch saw. You will also find a scroll saw, a portable radial arm saw, several miter and compound-miter saws, a jointer-planer, cordless tools, a random-orbit sander, belt and part-sheet sanders, drills, circular saws, jigsaws, routers and laminate trimmers, power-hand planers, a biscuit joiner, and more. Ryobi also makes a chisel mortiser, one of only three companies I know of to do so, a chain mortiser. and many other tools. The Ryobi catalog and product literature is free, on request.

S-B Power Tool Co.
4300 W. Peterson Avenue
Chicago, IL 60646
Attention: Marketing Communications
(312) 286–7330

S-B Power Tool Company combines Skil Corporation and Bosch Tools to form a true marketing giant with a wide line of tools sold through hardware stores, home centers, lumberyards, and woodworking outlets. *Skilsaw* became almost a generic term for circular saw. (The company fights this association like the devil. It's flattering to be so closely tied to a tool your company brought out first, but in later years, it's also limiting.) S-B Power Tool Company is now noted for a full line of corded and cordless portable power tools, and has recently developed a line of bench-top stationary tools—a table saw, drill press, disc-belt sander, scroll saw, and bench grinder. Their Top Gun 12-volt cordless drill is known as one of the top models in that field. Since Skil joined with Bosch some interesting changes have been made in the tool lines of both companies. Ask for brochures.

Stanley-Bostitch Fastening Systems
Route 2, Briggs Drive
East Greenwich, RI 02818
(800) 556–6696 or
(401) 884–2500
Fax (401) 884–2485

Stanley-Bostitch air nailers are handy even in the home workshop. Most useful to woodworkers are the brad and finishing nailers, though shop construction is a lot easier with framing nailers. Stanley-Bostitch is one of the top-of-the-line brands, and as such is a bit higher priced than some others, but the prices aren't out of line, given the quality of the tools. The company also makes its own line of high-powered, small air compressors. Call or write for information.

Stanley Tools
600 Myrtle Street
New Britain, CT 06050
(203) 225–5111
Fax (203) 827–5829

Any carpenter who is not at least minimally familiar with the Stanley tool line has been on another planet. Call or write for further information on hammers, screwdrivers, planes, chisels, awls, nail sets, and much, much more. The $4.00 full-line catalog will stun you with the width and breadth of the Stanley line, but the free *Contractor Grade Tool* catalog and the new *Fine Woodworking and Specialty Tool* catalog, also free, will be more useful to most of us. The new wood gouges and chisels from Stanley are cases in point: The hardwood handles are hopped at the top to withstand heavy use. Stanley's new top-of-the line wood chisels are made in Sheffield, England, from specially hardened ball-bearing steel. Bailey planes have returned to Stanley, with fine, gray cast-iron bases and simple adjustments for plane iron alignment, cut depth, and mouth size. The venerable Yankee ratcheting screwdriver is also back, something I'm glad to see, as much as I love cordless drills. Stanley tools are available in just about every outlet in the country, but a call or note to Stanley will bring a copy of either of the free catalogs.

Tool Crib of the North
Box 1716
Grand Forks, ND 58206
(800) 358–3096
Fax (701) 746–2857

The colorful Tool Crib catalog shows a wide, wide range of tools, from the AccuMiter to Vega fence systems, with in-between listings for Black and Decker, Freud, Milwaukee, Porter-Cable, Makita, Delta, General, S-K, Vise-Grip, HTC, Porta-Nails (PNI), Ridgid, Jet, Shop-Vac, Elu, DeWalt, Ryobi, and many more. Products include levels, jigs, HVLP sprayers, and glues. Tool Crib accepts Discover, Mastercard, and Visa.

Trend-Lines
375 Beacham Street
Chelsea, MA 02150
Orders (800) 767–9999
Customer service (800) 877–7899
Fax (617) 853–0226

Trend-Lines is a discount mail-order house and the distributor of the Reliant line of power tools. Their catalog includes Dremel, Delta, Ryobi, Panasonic, Black and Decker, Bostitch, Campbell-Hausfeld, Fuji (HVLP), Freud, Nikon, Record, Marples, Grant, Porter-Cable, Makita, ITW-Paslode, Senco, DML, PNI, Oldham, Performax, and a slew of others. Their free catalog presents more than 3,000 brand-name products, including power tools and accessories, hand tools, screws, hardware, wood parts, plans, and books. It emphasizes tools, including roller work stations, a new, industrial-style 10-inch table saw, Porter-Cable's new Laser Loc 10-inch miter saw (an item I've recently tried: that fast, moving either-side-of-the-blade laser line *really* puts you on your mark), and much of the new DeWalt line of portable power tools. The company also sells raised panels for drawer fronts and doors, dowels, wood-threading kits, and glues. Complete satisfaction is guaranteed. Trend-Lines accepts Mastercard, Visa, and American Express.

Trojan Manufacturing, Inc.
9810 N. Vancouver Way
Portland, OR 97217
(800) 745–2120
Fax (503) 285–7731

Trojan Manufacturing produces a variety of carpentry aides. The Rip Master takes a lightweight table saw, increases ripping capacity to 28 inches, and makes that saw easily portable: It folds down and forms a cart for transport, but supports the saw securely when unfolded. Ten-inch-diameter wheels make all sorts of job site transport easy. Also of interest to the woodworker is the work center miter saw stand. This stand has two sets of legs, accepts a 2-x-6-inch center bar, and has two roller supports to fit at the ends of the 2 x 6. Miter saws and compound miter saws become more useful when well supported. Trojan also makes a strong series of metal sawhorse legs in two heights (27 and 35 inches) that assemble easily and quickly. Call for free brochures. Trojan sells through 3,000 dealers but also sells direct. They accept Mastercard and Visa.

Whole Earth Access
822 Anthony Street
Berkeley, CA 94710
(800) 829–6300
Fax (510) 845–8846

Whole Earth Access offers what they call the best tools on earth, the Elu line (from Black and Decker), which has turned into an elite, hard-to-find in the United States line of tools. Whole Earth also sells other tools and offers free freight within the continental United States. Give them a call for up-to-date price lists and brochures. Whole Earth accepts Discover, Mastercard, and Visa.

SOURCES OF INFORMATION

National Association of Home Builders
(202) 822–0216

NAHB has a great many books, brochures, and other items that are of interest. The NAHB offers a Certificate Graduate Remodeler program among other educational opportunities. They're located in the Washington, D.C., area.

National Association of the Remodeling Industry
(703) 276–7600

The NARI offers a guide to state licensing requirements in all fifty states. They also offer a line of books and brochures that can be of great help. They're located in northern Virginia.

Once you begin to employ more than twenty-five people, you'll find OSHA (Occupational Safety and Health Administration) has varying requirements for different workplaces. Rather than going directly to the federal horse's mouth, check with your local home builders association for information and help on meeting OSHA regulations, providing written hazard communications for employees, and similar needs.

Marshall & Swift
P.O. Box 26307
Los Angeles, CA 90026
(800) 544-2678

Marshall & Swift offers the *Dodge Repair and Remodel Cost Book* and Repair & Remodel Estimator, a computer program that features more than 1,200 component costs and also provides location summaries, component reports, work summaries, detail reports, and bid reports. They offer a free demonstration disk.

Wil McKnight Associates
207 West Jefferson Street
Bloomington, IN 61701
(309) 829-5329

Construction Supervisor is the name of a helpful book from McKnight.

Craftsman Book Company
P.O. Box 6500
Carlsbad, CA 92018
(800) 829-8123

Craftsman has an extensive line of books and computer programs, including *Construction Estimating Reference Data* (book), that includes DataEst, a free disk with estimating features; National Construction Estimator, including 30,000 labor and material cost estimates on disk; *Daily Job Log* for deliveries, changes, completions, deadlines, inspections, due dates, and others; and *Drafting House Plans,* a book to get anyone up and running on drawing house plans.

Journal of Light Construction Bookstore
Box 698
Mt. Morris, IL 61054
(800) 375–5981

This specialty bookstore offers titles such as *Kitchens & Baths: A Builders' Guide To Design & Construction; Techniques, Troubleshooting and Structural Design; Basic Engineering for Builders; Architectural Plans for Adding On or Remodeling; Construction Forms & Contracts; Contractor's Guide to The Building Code;* and many others.

Linden Publishing
3845 North Blackstone Avenue
Fresno, CA 93276
(800) 345–4447

Linden prints new books and reprints old classics, including Ellis' *Modern Practical Joinery.*

Vintage Wood Works
Highway 34, Box R, #2762
Quinlan, TX 75474
(903) 356–2158

VWW offers *Porches: How To Design, Build & Decorate,* and a catalog of architectural details for Victorian and country looks.

SOFTWARE

For those of you interested in looking at more computer programs, here's a short list of available items, including an easy-to-use computer-aided-design (CAD) program, estimating software, a forms disk, and a list of general business programs.

SDSI Business Systems
27475 Ynez Road, Suite 385
Temecula, CA 92591
(800) 872–7165

SDSI offers Windows and DOS versions of Estimate Writer, which features a modifiable 30,000-item database. Retail price is about $50.

SoftPlan Systems, Inc.
214 Overlook Court, Suite 220
Brentwood, TN 37027
(800) 248–0164

SoftPlan offers a free demo disk of their SoftPlan CAD software, specifically designed to ease the job of producing floor plans, roof designs, elevations, cross-sections, materials lists, and cost estimates.

WinEstimator, Inc
(800) 950–2374

This company offers Estimating for Windows, a full-featured estimating program that sells for less than $500.

Wilhelm Publishing, Inc.
P.O. Box 922
Columbia, MO 65205
(Fax) (800) 875–5114

Wilhelm sells sixty-three construction forms and contracts that work with most major word processors. Documents include builder contracts (lump-sum fee, remodel fee); subcontractor contracts (framing, electrical, etc.); estimate forms; cost worksheets; change orders; cost-plus and fixed-price forms; house, room addition, kitchen, bathroom and basement spec forms; warranty, sixty-day, and one-year check forms; and many others.

Scale-Link™
Scalex Corporation
2794 Loker Avenue West, Suite 105
Carlsbad, CA 92008
(800) 653–3532

Scale-Link is an OCR (optical character reader) that picks up figures from columns and other tight spots and enters them directly into estimating and spreadsheet programs.

Soft A'Ware Publishing Company
8057 Raytheon Road, Suite 4
San Diego, CA 92111
(800) 655–4799

Soft A'Ware offers an array of shareware software. For about $5.00 a disk, you'll get spreadsheets, vehicle history and maintenance programs, contract keepers, and more. Some are well worth considering, some are less so, but many are interesting.

Eagle Point
4131 Westmark Drive
Dubuque, IA 52002
(800) 678–6565
Fax (319) 556–5321

Eagle Point offers top-end estimating software.

MAGAZINES AND ASSOCIATIONS

There are many publications and organizations that can help the start-up carpenter/builder/cabinetmaker. You've seen several of the magazines on the newsstand, like *Fine Homebuilding,* and already know the kind of detailed how-to information they can provide for tool selection and use and for building techniques. The selection of specialized, controlled circulation publications known as trade magazines is much larger, and presents a different picture: Magazines such as *Building & Remodeling News* present information on new techniques, materials, computers and pro-grams, and just about anything else associated with small building con-tractors. They seldom provide how-to information, but do publish exhaustive tool tests and cover areas of interest such as the handling of solid-surface countertop materials, including Corian and a few others.

Other publications, including *Rural Builder, The Journal of Light Construction* (a recent issue of which instructs in installing sprinkler systems, fast fas-cia installation, window trim for thick walls, and new kinds of pneumatic fasteners), *Tools of the Trade, Frame Building News* (official publication of the National Frame Building Association), and *Woodshop News* provide out-looks on different aspects of the builder's trade. These publications are aimed at the professional builder, and their how-to articles are of great value.

Builder magazine, official publication of the National Association of Home Builders, gives a view of what's going on in the association. This book can't list your local contractors' associations because there are too many, and you must judge the merits of the local ones yourself. The NAHB, though, helps you keep up-to-date on national trends, as do most of the other magazines. *Building & Remodeling News* is a special case, oper-ating a number of regional editions with material aimed at builders in those areas. Some of those magazines are available on newsstands; others are mailed free to building professionals. Some are given only to members of the particular association involved.

Builder
National Association of Home Builders
655 15th Street N.W., #475
Washington, D.C. 20005
(202 737–0717 (for information on NAHB, and the requirements and fees for joining)

Building & Remodeling News
600-C Lake Street
Ramsey, NJ 07446
(201) 327–1600
Free to contractors in circulation area

Fine Homebuilding
Taunton Press
Newtown, CT 06470
(203) 426–8171
Available on newsstands or by subscription

Frame Building News
National Frame Builders Association
4849 W. 15th Street, Suite 1000
Lawrenceville, KS 66049

Journal of Light Construction
RR2 Box 146
Richmond, VT 05477
(800) 375–5981

Professional Builder
Cahners Publishing Co.
1350 E. Touhy
Des Plaines, IL 60018
(708) 390–2111
Free to builders

Rural Builder
700 East State Street
Iola, WI 54990
(715) 445–4612, ext. 257
Free to rural builders

Tools of the Trade
RR2 Box 146
Richmond, VT 05477
(800) 375–5981

Woodshop News
Soundings Publications
35 Pratt Street
Essex, CT 06426
$15.97 per year

CREDIT APPLICATION

Application No.
Company:
Company Address:
Telephone:
Fax:
Type of Business (Partnership. Corp.):
Years in Business:

PARTNERS OR CORPORATE OFFICERS

Name	Title	Telephone

BANK REFERENCES

Bank Name & Address	Contact Name & Phone	Account Number(s)

TRADE REFERENCES

I certify that the above information is true. This information is to be used only for opening an account.

Signature	Title	Date

EXPENSES AND INCOME ACCOUNTING SHEET

Account Name:

Date	Source or Item	Amount	Total for Month	Year Cumulative Total

QUARTERLY CASH FLOW

	1st	2nd	3rd	4th
Operating Activities				
Net Cash Provided/Used By Operating Activities				
Investing Activities	$	$	$	$
Net Cash Provided/Used By Operating Activities				
Financing/Activities	$	$	$	$
Net Cash Provided/Used By Operating Activities				
Net Increase/Decrease in Cash				
Cash and Equivalents at Beginning of Quarter				
Cash and Equivalents at end of Quarter				

BIBLIOGRAPHY

Fallek, Max. *How to Set Up Your Own Small Business,* American Institute of Small Business, 2 volumes, 1987.

Gerstel, David. *The Builder's Guide to Running a Successful Construction Company,* Taunton Press, 1991.

Lasser, J.K., Institute. *How to Run a Small Business,* McGraw-Hill, 1994.

Oberrecht, Kenn. *How to Open and Operate a Home-Based Photography Business,* The Globe Pequot Press, Inc., 1993.

INDEX

vehicles. See automobiles/vehicles

waste of materials, allowing for,
  126
Windows, 24
word-of-mouth advertising, 61–62
worker's compensation, 54

work week, number of hours
  needed, 2

Yellow Pages, advertising in, 55

zoning issues, 12–15

ABOUT THE AUTHOR

CHARLES SELF is a full-time freelance writer who has also worked as a carpenter for the past twenty-five years. He has written more than thirty-five books, many on carpentry and woodworking, and more than 1,000 magazine and newspaper articles on related subjects. He makes his home in Bedford, Virginia.